MW01445164

The Superstar Curriculum

D'Arcie & Marley,

Your greatest moments await!

Happy reading,

The Superstar Curriculum

How to Shine in School and Create Your Brightest Future

Second Edition

Ryan Keliher
BA, BEd, MBA

© 2016, 2018 Ryan Keliher
All rights reserved. This book or any portion thereof may not be reproduced or used in any manner whatsoever without the express written permission of the publisher except for the use of brief quotations in a book review.

ISBN-13: 9781728669779

*I dedicate this book to those who believe that
the brightest tomorrow begins today.*

The stories in this book are all true, but names have been changed to respect the privacy of individuals.

Table of Contents

About the Book · xi
Redefining *Superstar* · xv

The Four Stages of Superstardom

Stage 1—Develop Your Character
1 Value First Impressions · 5
2 Be a Class Act · 9
3 Understand the Power of Perception · · · · · · · · · · · · · · · · · 13
4 Know That You Are Part of Something Bigger · · · · · · · · · · 18
5 Get to Know the Friends Who Aren't Your Friends · · · · · · 22
6 Be Good to Everyone · 27
7 Be a Goal Setter · 32

Stage 2—Develop Your Mind
8 Hone Your Work Ethic · 39
9 Develop Resilience Daily · 44
10 Discover the Importance of Persistence · · · · · · · · · · · · · · · 49
11 Make Friends with Momentum · 53
12 Succeed through Sacrifice · 57
13 Accept Challenges and Responsibilities · · · · · · · · · · · · · · · 62
14 Ignite Your Internal Motivation · 66

Stage 3—Develop Your Opportunities
15   Understand Opportunity Cost · 73
16   Treasure Your Time · 78
17   Make Room for Reading · 82
18   Value Volunteerism · 87
19   Learn Effective Listening · 91
20   Step Out of Your Comfort Zone · · · · · · · · · · · · · · · · · · 95
21   Never Stop Learning · 99

Stage 4—Develop Your Leadership
22   Believe in Yourself · 107
23   Don't Let Your Past Define You · · · · · · · · · · · · · · · · · · 111
24   Be Better Than You Were Yesterday · · · · · · · · · · · · · · · 115
25   "Don't Worry, Be Happy" · 119
26   Be True to You · 124
27   Be Inspirational · 128
28   Create Positive Change · 132

About the Book

Your biggest opportunity may be right where you are now.

—Napoleon Hill

Thank you for picking up *The Superstar Curriculum*. I hope this book positively changes your approach to learning and life. Did you know that you invest over ten thousand hours in school by the time you graduate? That's a tremendous commitment of precious time. Over the past eleven years as a teacher, I've seen too many students view their time in school as an obligation rather than an opportunity, and I could no longer merely watch this happen. Your life is too valuable. I wrote this book because I want you to receive maximum benefit from the significant number of hours you invest.

Education should focus more on growth than grades, yet every year there are graduates, including the highest achievers, who finish school still unaware of specific skills, habits, or attitudes that need further development—ones that would significantly improve their lives and futures. When school systems are preoccupied with assessing academic curricular content, valuable lessons about everyday success principles too often go unaddressed. **The most exceptional qualities and habits you can develop in school are often not explicitly taught in class, but the opportunities to develop them are abundant.** The fundamental skills highlighted in this book will help you stand out in an increasingly competitive world.

If you choose to adopt the concepts of this curriculum, a multitude of development opportunities beyond actual schoolwork will begin to blossom in front of you each day. Much like hockey legend Wayne Gretzky's ability to see scoring chances develop before anyone else on the ice, after reading this book, you will see opportunities in school where others may not. These opportunities, once seized, will set you up for a lifetime of personal growth and fulfillment. And, like Gretzky, not only will your ability to recognize and embrace such moments lead to your own success, but your efforts will help strengthen those around you. You'll be become a leader through your actions.

If you glance in the mirror right now, you should already see twinkles of superstardom in your eyes. Various chapters will reinforce remarkable traits that you already possess, while others will highlight areas for improvement. The goal is to develop the full package. There are optional *Reflection and Self-Awareness* opportunities at the end of each chapter. Answering the questions will help you tailor the book's advice to your life. Purposeful reflection prompts your thinking; your thinking ignites action; your actions create habits; and your habits deliver results. Self-awareness is critical to this book and vital to your progress. Each chapter should challenge your mind and encourage you to evaluate past actions, recognize future opportunities, and provoke positive change.

Although some of the chapters are interconnected, you can read this book any which way—front to back, back to front, or starting in the middle. All sections are short (I know how busy teenagers are these days). You could tackle one chapter per day, taking roughly ten minutes, and change your life in less than a month. I tried to write the book I wish I could've had as a teenager. While I am an optimist, I am also a realist. I do not expect that every teenager will take the time and effort to read this book and employ its teachings, which further reinforces my decision to title it *The Superstar Curriculum*. Superstars are willing to do what most won't. Here is a chance for you to launch yourself into rare air. Success takes time, and your time starts now.

Redefining *Superstar*

You are braver than you believe, stronger than you seem, and smarter than you think.

—A. A. Milne

Christopher Robin said the above to his beloved furry friend Winnie-the-Pooh; those two timeless characters brought out the best in each other. They were superstars in each other's lives. Take a moment to think deeply about the most prominent superstar in your life. Do you have someone in mind?

The first time I performed this exercise with a group of students, I was surprised when not one person envisioned a celebrity as the biggest superstar. Parents, siblings, relatives, friends, teachers, and coaches made up much of the list. While famous people can definitely serve as incredible sources of inspiration, the results of this activity emphasized the profound power we have to influence those around us on a daily basis. True superstars live everywhere. In fact, you are a superstar; you just might not know it…yet.

Forget fortune and fame—the world's most respected people, no matter their craft and notoriety, share a common attribute that I call the **superstar mindset: a genuine desire to develop and contribute.** Whether you speak of Mother Teresa or Michael Jordan, family members or friends, or musicians or mechanics, those who seek to better themselves and help in meaningful ways will see positive results, gain respect, and become sources of inspiration in life. So cool, so admirable, and best of all, so possible.

Schools are filled with superstar potential but are not filled with superstars, which is a big problem that this little book can solve. The ideas presented in this book will help you cultivate qualities that put you in high demand and even higher regard. You will sharpen your skill set and brighten each room you enter. Once you adopt the superstar mindset, more and more you will create moments in your life where you are living kindly, learning continuously, and contributing meaningfully. The more of these moments you create, the better your life will become, both now and in the future.

Come graduation night, when you walk across the stage to accept your diploma, people will be thinking, "That person is going to wow people wherever he or she goes in life." Superstars are in the business of wowing people, and, in turn, people love rooting for and connecting with superstars. Once you have a genuine desire to develop and contribute, new windows of opportunity will begin flying open for you. Are you ready? It's time to transform from student to superstar.

Superstar Mindset:
A genuine desire to develop and contribute

The Four Stages of Superstardom

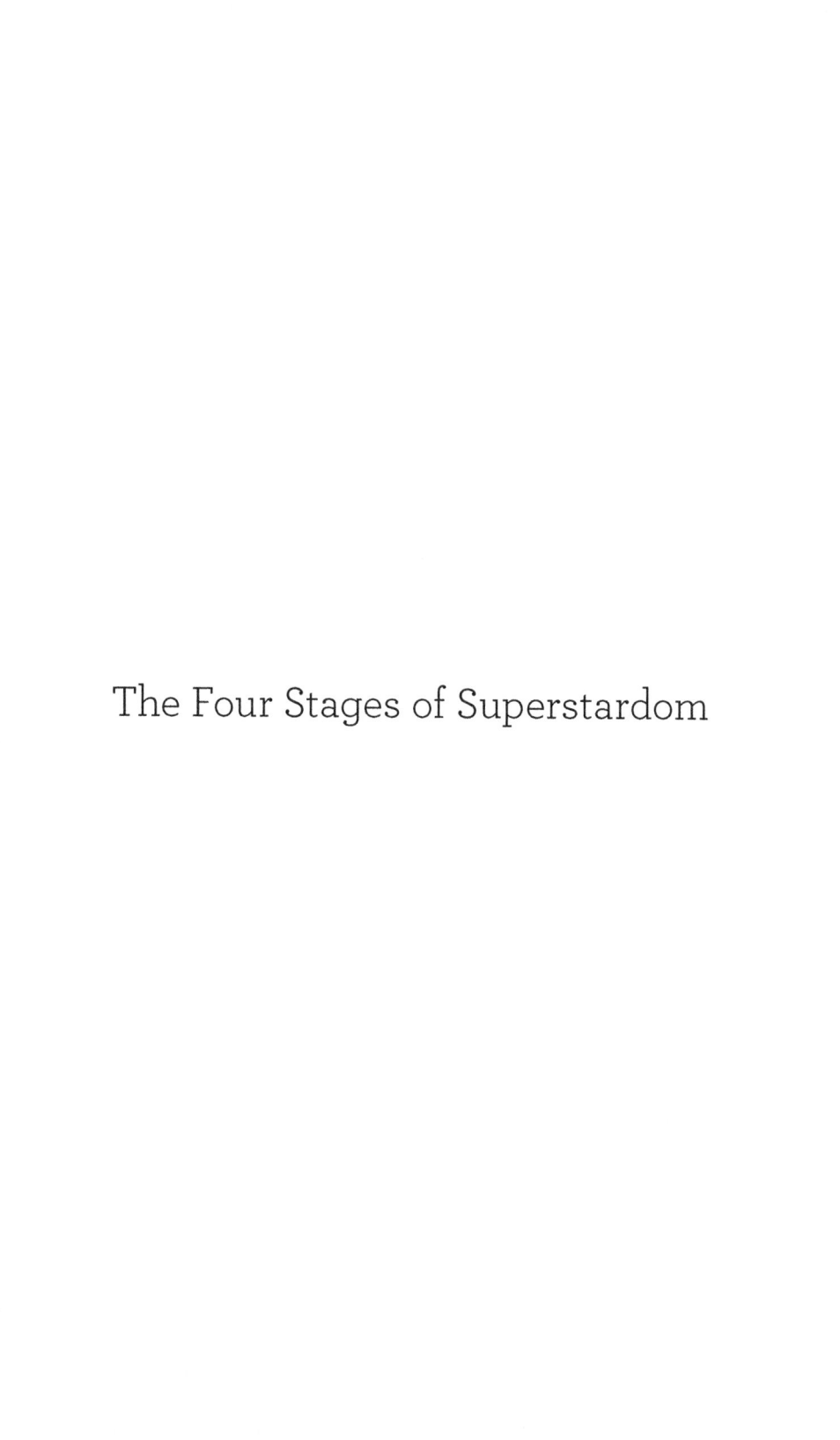

Stage 1
Develop Your Character

Intelligence plus character—that is the goal of true education.

—Martin Luther King Jr.

In order to reach your potential, you need strong moral and mental qualities. This stage focuses on developing principled habits that will strengthen your personal character, improve the quality of your relationships, and enhance your ability to contribute in meaningful ways.

1

Value First Impressions

A good first impression can work wonders.

—J. K. ROWLING

YOU ONLY EVER get one chance at a first impression. At the beginning of every semester, I meet approximately one hundred new students. The first day is always a blur, but I always remember the handful of students who make positive first impressions. I also often recall the few students who make negative first impressions. And I forget the rest (I eventually get to know them, I promise). People can form opinions about you—good or bad, right or wrong—within the first few moments of meeting you. When these first impressions do occur, they often last, so let the best version of you shine when meeting someone for the first time. Valuing first encounters is an easy way to stand out for all the right reasons.

Making a compelling first impression can be simple. A few years ago, a student approached me after the first day of class, and with a smile on his face, he said, "It was nice meeting you today. See you tomorrow." He likely would not even remember our little interaction, but it was genuine, kind, and so rare that it made a lasting impression on me. Never underestimate how significantly even the smallest positive act can impact others. His actions weren't fake, nor were they excessive or elaborate. I appreciated the kind gesture, and for the rest of the year, I thought highly of this student. I enjoyed seeing him walk through the door each day, and there's no doubt that our memorable yet straightforward first encounter was a big reason why.

School provides you with opportunities to make positive first impressions on teachers, crushes, classmates—the list goes on. Here are some ways to help you knock your next first impression out of the park:

- Be yourself. The best first impressions are authentic.
- Greet people. Smiling and introducing yourself helps people feel comfortable, safe, and at ease.
- Participate. Listening intently, using positive body language, and asking questions move conversations forward and show that you genuinely care about the interaction.
- Be punctual. Or, when you're late, give an explanation. In school, teachers love when you speak to them.
- Come prepared. This demonstrates responsibility. Would you go to play tennis without caring that you forgot your racket? It should be the same in the classroom with supplies.
- Respect rules. You'll never go wrong by showing respect. And if you don't agree with a particular rule, have a conversation with someone in charge instead of immediately defying it.

These simple actions give off friendly, warm vibes. People like warm vibes (that's why hot yoga is so popular). If you forget the suggestions listed above, just be genuinely kind. **The best kind of person is a kind person.** Later in life, you will meet people for the first time in various important moments. You will meet your future girlfriend or boyfriend, husband or wife, colleagues and bosses, and teammates and friends. Using school to develop the habit of creating positive first impressions will make these always-important-but-often-stressful situations easier.

Deliberately making a positive first impression will improve your social environments by garnering mutual respect. If you put your best self forward, your recipients will appreciate your actions and give you their best back. They will feel valued and look forward to future interactions. The next time you encounter somebody, whether it is a classmate or a cashier, be the type of person you'd like to meet (not only will this strategy help you make a great impression, but it's also a simple way to build self-confidence). Positive first impressions lead to positive relationships, so approach each new encounter like a star and shine brightly. You will develop relationships that are out of this world.

Reflection and Self-Awareness Opportunity

1) How effective are you at making positive first impressions? Which tips from the chapter have you employed in the past? Which tip could you improve upon?

2) Create a list of people you could try to make a positive impression on in your life:
   1.
   2.
   3.

3) How could you go about creating these positive first impressions?
   1.
   2.
   3.

2

Be a Class Act

Kind words are short and easy to speak, but their echoes are truly endless.

—Mother Teresa

We all know the importance of minding our manners, and although being polite sounds easy in theory, developing any superstar habit involves conscious effort and concerted practice. Back in eleventh grade, I had a teacher who told my class that manners could get us just as far in life as good grades. I figured it was her way of getting us to behave, but over time I have come to understand and appreciate her advice. When you are polite, people like you. People are more willing to help you. It honestly is that simple. Good manners can open doors for you that other skills and characteristics cannot.

Your manners, or lack thereof, become an extension of you. Words help create and reveal your character, so be mindful of your vocabulary. Buddha suggested that "before you speak, ask yourself if what you are going to say is true, is kind, is necessary, is helpful. If the answer is no, maybe what you are about to say should be left unsaid." Make a habit of using terms associated with respect. Even simple words, such as *hello, goodbye, please,* and *thank you,* are always appreciated, no matter if you are speaking to a best friend or a bus driver. When you use positive language, both verbal and nonverbal, the people with whom you interact will feel better about you and themselves. School is an excellent environment in which to make good manners part of your identity because of the many social interactions that occur there every day. In the halls or at your locker, you will see people, bump into people, and cut people off accidentally. Be polite in those situations; say hi, excuse me, or sorry. Greeting others and responding well to greetings brings a refreshing aura of respect into the world.

Being polite is also a low-risk way to socialize positively. Manners can give naturally quiet people a voice in social situations and can serve as a springboard to launch further conversation. Manners also have a way of softening the boom of overtly outgoing individuals. When you are genuinely polite, people are more likely to form favorable opinions of you. As already discussed, first impressions are so important, and good manners only help in this regard by making you more social, respectful, and memorable.

While your words can be powerful, your actions speak even louder. Polite people help others, listen when someone talks, and are mindful in social situations. For instance, if you are always pumping music through your earbuds in public, then it's hard to give someone your full attention. There's a time and a place for everything. And yes, sometimes having your earbuds in is the polite thing to do (you almost got me there). The same goes for using your smartphone in social situations. Always think about how your actions might affect others, and act the way you want to be seen and treated. Be the person who holds a door open for friends and strangers. Be a role model around children. Be the first to smile and say hello. These actions will create positive reactions. You will develop more meaningful relationships and contribute to a better social environment.

Developing good manners in school will help generate benefits in other aspects of your life. Thoughtful words and actions can help you get a job or get a date, then help you again in your job and on your date. You can impress your boyfriend's or girlfriend's parents, get better service at a restaurant or hotel, and the list goes on. Using sincere manners at a given moment shows that you are fully present. People appreciate that—in an era where extreme distraction is literally at our fingertips, being fully present in the moment is becoming increasingly rare. Allow your manners to demonstrate that you are a refined individual who values the presence of others.

Tomorrow, track the words you use and the actions you display. World-class companies are exceptionally mindful of their word choice, and they pride themselves on their customer service. You can do the same. Choose respectful words and actions that strengthen your personal brand and lift others up. People will enjoy your positive presence, and as a result, you'll enjoy richer interactions.

Five years or even twenty years from now, an opportunity might arise for you because of the way you treated someone today. Your actions can impact others long after an interaction ends. And although our society seems to place tremendous emphasis on aesthetics, always focus more on how you act than how you look. **The clothes you wear won't always remain popular, but the good manners you demonstrate will always be in style.** Everyone loves a classic.

Reflection and Self-Awareness Opportunity

1) When it comes to your manners (respectful words and actions), circle the statement that best applies to you:
   a) I am often not a polite person and do not mind my manners.
   b) I am a polite person, but my manners could use some work.
   c) I am a polite person but am more quiet than anything.
   d) I am a polite person, and my manners demonstrate respect.

2) List times when you could practice or improve upon your manners during the run of a school day:
   a)
   b)
   c)

3) Think about the types of words you use on a daily basis. How do they reflect your personal brand?

4) Try tracking your words and actions for a day. After doing so, what did you notice?

3

Understand the Power of Perception

Some people feel the rain while others just get wet.

—Bob Marley

I once coached a player who always found herself in foul trouble during basketball games. After a referee would signal a foul, she'd often turn to me, exclaiming, "But coach, I didn't foul her." What she failed to realize was that once the whistle blew, whether she had indeed fouled her opponent no longer mattered because the situation was about perception. The reality for the referee was that a foul had been committed, yet the truth for her was that no foul had occurred. Could they both have been right? Not really, but maybe a little bit. You see, people's perceptions of things often shape their versions of the truth. The sooner you understand this reality, the better your life will become.

Reality differs for everybody. For instance, you may view yourself or your peer group in one light, while others might share a completely different opinion. Sometimes versions of reality match up, and sometimes they don't. For this reason, it is essential to understand that others can and will perceive your behaviors, attitudes, and actions in ways that shape their reality.

Always consider how you are presenting yourself in a given moment. If you seem lazy, someone will perceive you as lazy. If you appear kind, someone will view you as kind. If you come across as rude, defiant, or irresponsible (you get the point), others will see you as such. I'm not suggesting that you should always seek others' approval or constantly worry about what others think of you—that's not healthy—but you should be mindful of your reputation. Rightly or wrongly, it follows you. You can use school as a social and academic platform to build a reputation based on commendable actions you display. Understanding how these actions help form your reputation can encourage you to make decisions that better shape people's opinions. This is especially true with your online presence. Be aware of how you portray yourself through both pictures and words online via social platforms. Your digital footprint, good or bad, is long lasting (and unforgiving when negative). In our technological society, first impressions often occur online, so always remember how someone else could interpret your online actions. By considering the way you'd like to be perceived, you will improve your reality.

* * *

Just as it's important to understand that others will create their versions of reality based on perception, it's also important to understand how perception can frame your version of reality. Henry Ford, founder of Ford Motor Company and superstar innovator, put it best when he said, "Whether you think you can, or you think you can't—you're right." If you believe that you cannot achieve something, the truth is that you likely will not accomplish it. If you view your life as negative, then cynical energy will fuel your days. But if you believe that something is achievable, it will more likely become a reality. Your thoughts drive your actions. **Changing your outlook can change your life.** Think about this: if you can change your mind, which we do all the time, then you can change your mindset. Your thoughts are powerful, for they dictate how you see and interact with the world around you. Optimism breeds opportunity. Using the immense power of your mind to perceive each day positively will create an abundance of opportunity in your life.

When you learn to focus on your possibilities instead of your problems, anything becomes achievable. Superstar tennis champion Roger Federer served up the right idea when he said, "I think I am great; therefore, I am." Allow your perception to lift you instead of limit you. Too often we build imaginary walls that confine our lives. Far too many students limit themselves personally, academically, and socially because of their life circumstances, past experiences, or personal doubts. Break down these walls, and find the courage to explore an existence where anything is possible. Think like Federer, and understand that you are capable of incredible feats. Never let your perception overpower your potential. With the right mindset, you can perform beyond your wildest dreams and lift others up along the way. Friends will admire your positive outlook and turn to you for support and inspiration. If you try to become a person you'd love, then you'll love the person you'll become. And everyone else will love you too.

In summary, your perception will help create your future reality. Imagine a world where everyone wears glasses, and each prescription represents a person's perception of things. Always be aware of how you might look through someone else's lenses, and when it comes to your prescription, make sure you get regular checkups. When your vision starts limiting you, get a new pair of glasses that allow you to refocus on all the wondrous possibilities that exist. Where one fellow sees dirt, the farmer sees opportunity. How beautiful is that?

Reflection and Self-Awareness Opportunity

1) How do you think others generally perceive your actions, attitudes, and behaviors in school?
   a) Negatively
   b) Somewhat negatively
   c) Hard to say
   d) Somewhat positively
   e) Positively

If you answered A, B, or C, write down some changes you could make in your life to improve others' perceptions of you.

2) What is your current perception of life?
   a) Negative
   b) Somewhat negative
   c) Haven't really thought about it
   d) Somewhat positive
   e) Positive

If you answered A, B, or C, try writing down three positive aspects of your life. Remember, changing your outlook on life will change your life.

3) What are some imaginary walls that you've built for yourself? What are some potential benefits of breaking down these walls?

4

Know That You Are Part of Something Bigger

It is our collective and individual responsibility to preserve and tend to the environment in which we all live.

—Dalai Lama

It's astounding how many varied networks exist in our lives. In all these different circles, we are the common denominators, so it's often easy to think of our own interests first. It's necessary to realize, however, that we are always part of something much bigger than ourselves. This understanding brings an attitude of collective responsibility. By embracing our capacity to affect others positively, we often make better decisions and, in doing so, change the world for the better. That's a rewarding way to live.

In your life today, some of your various networks could include

- your family;
- your friend groups;
- your school;
- your work;
- your sports team, band, or other clubs and groups;
- your neighborhood, town, or city;
- your province, state, or country; and
- your world.

Your actions help create these networks. School, which is a community of its own, allows you to become part of something bigger because it's a place where small actions impact a large group. For example, if all students left their waste at the cafeteria table after eating lunch, what kind of mess would it create? Now extend this cafeteria example to our precious planet. Scary, I know, but that is how collective responsibility works. Thinking of personal convenience ahead of collective responsibility often results in shortsighted judgments, bad decisions, and potential negative consequences for yourself and others. Instead, when the motivation for our actions is to serve others, the result is that we also best serve ourselves.

Your environment is more than physical; it's also social. Communication and collaboration skills are some of the most highly regarded skills for your generation, so capitalize on these developmental opportunities in school. Unfortunately, when working in a group, many students fail to do their fair share, knowing that others will eventually pick up their slack. Don't be one of those people. If you make selfish choices (ones where you think primarily of personal benefit), then the collective whole, of which you are a part, suffers. Whether you are working as a group in class, as part of a team, or as a member of your family, know that your attitude, work ethic, and actions will affect others. Always hold up your end of the bargain. Group experiences where everyone produces at their highest levels will create some of your most memorable moments and rewarding results. Legendary football coach Vince Lombardi said, "Individual commitment to a group effort—that is what makes a team work, a company work, a society work, and a civilization work." Developing your commitment levels will help you contribute to your various groups in meaningful ways. Putting forth your finest effort is a perfect way to lead by example. The world needs more of these everyday leaders working together; that's how the biggest problems are solved. **Mindful people, committed to a greater cause, refine the world.**

If you envision a world where everyone understands that they are part of something bigger, you will see the world as a beautiful place with infinite potential. Imagine if everyone went out of their way to help others, if everyone made more personal sacrifices for the greater good, if everyone wore seat belts and decided never to drink and drive. What if everyone stopped being hurtful because they understood how their words and actions negatively affected others? If you, just you, recognize the collective power of carrying out these individual acts, your environments will benefit. You'll drive positive change and inspire others to make the world a better place—that's superstar material.

PS: Read or listen to the news to inform yourself of the bigger picture. It's unfortunate that mostly negative news is broadcast, but hearing it can reframe your life with a fresh perspective. When you concern yourself with the well-being of others as much as you do your own, you will realize some of your problems might be more manageable than you first thought. Developing empathy for others can lighten your own pain. Plus, how can you help solve the world's problems if you don't know they exist? The world needs you to care about it. We are all in this together. All right, hands in. *Team* on three.

Reflection and Self-Awareness Opportunity

1) Think of a group or network in which you are currently involved. Now think about your actions within the group. How have your actions affected the group?

   Group/Network:

   Actions:

   Effect:

2) What is an issue in your community, country, or world that is important to you? Do some research to learn more about it. See if you can help!

5

Get to Know the Friends Who Aren't Your Friends

Surround yourself with only people who are going to take you higher.

—Oprah Winfrey

Socializing is a valuable element of your total school experience. If you have a social circle where you feel happy, that's awesome. If you do not have a friend group that makes you happy, then what you have is an opportunity. And opportunities are fantastic too.

Depending on the size of your school, you could have hundreds or thousands of potential friends in your building. You won't become friends with everybody. In fact, you may even dislike some people, and not everyone will like you either. Don't stress it. We are not all compatible. But just because you can't be friends with everyone doesn't mean you can't be friendly to everyone. Interacting in a welcoming fashion is a sure way to improve your social circle, your life, and the lives of others. Triple win.

The best way to make a friend is to be one; that will never change. Do you remember meeting your first friend? How do you think that relationship started? Chances are that one of you was authentically friendly without judgment. The concept still works today, but unfortunately, many students go years without speaking to or smiling at one another—not because they dislike each other but because they don't know each other. When you think about this situation, it is circular logic. Students won't speak with certain people because they don't know them, yet the reason they don't know them is that they don't speak. This results in students forming opinions of people before ever understanding them. Judging others before knowing them likely says more about your character than it does about theirs.

Instead, take a chance on friendship, and allow relationships to develop over time. For two people to meet, someone must initiate communication. Let that someone be you. While this might take courage, the outcome can be incredible. Ben Cohen and Jerry Greenfield, cofounders of the ultra successful ice cream company Ben & Jerry's, first met by striking up a conversation in a seventh-grade gym class (and the rest is sweet, delicious history!). The person sitting beside you could become your best friend, significant other, or business partner you go on to make millions with, but only if you are willing to be a friend first. It's an exciting opportunity worth exploring.

You improve any environment when you recognize the existence and celebrate the differences of others. Imagine if everyone in your school were friendly and compassionate to people who weren't their "friends." These actions can take the form of greetings, smiles, or offers to help. You have the power to make the world a friendlier place—a better place. When you contribute positively to your social environment, you bring joy into the world, which in turn comes back to you. There's always someone who needs a friend. You can help lead the world to happiness. That's everyday superhero stuff right there.

* * *

It's important to look closely at your social circle to determine whether the people with whom you socialize are indeed your friends. Unfortunately, upon honest, thoughtful reflection, people sometimes realize that certain "friends" are not real friends at all.

It's sad seeing students whose social circles bring them down. People who envy you in negative ways, put you down, pressure you to do things you don't want to do, or pressure you against doing what you want to do are not true friends. If such people make up your social circle, speak with them and reestablish what friendship means. If they are true friends, things will improve. If they don't respect what you have to say, the truth is you may be better off without that relationship in your life. Leaving a social group and attempting to make new friends is easier said than done, but sometimes the smartest decisions you'll ever make will also be the toughest. Strength of relationships is a primary determinant of happiness. Your time and your life are too valuable for toxic relationships.

You become a combination of the people with whom you spend most of your time, so choose only the finest of friends. Real friends are trustworthy and proud of you. They lift you up, respect you, and encourage you to be yourself and follow your dreams. And as a friend, you should genuinely reciprocate those actions and sentiments. **The only thing better than having a friend who brings out the best in you is being that friend to others.** Boxing superstar Muhammad Ali said, "Friendship...is not something you learn in school. But if you haven't learned the meaning of friendship, you really haven't learned anything." A school is a place where friendships develop, so use the opportunity to learn about one of life's most precious bonds. If you surround yourself with real friends, one day you'll look back on your life with countless memories of time shared with people you love. That sounds pretty good to me, my friend.

Reflection and Self-Awareness Opportunity

1) How comfortable do you feel talking to people who aren't your "friends"?
   a) Not comfortable at all
   b) Somewhat comfortable
   c) Comfortable
   d) Very comfortable

Write down an opportunity when you could reach out to someone who is not your "friend."

2) Think about your core group of friends. Are you happy with the people you are surrounding yourself with? Why or why not?

3) Think about the way you treat your core group of friends. Do you act how a true friend should? Why or why not?

6

Be Good to Everyone

*No matter what happens in life, be good to people.
Being good to people is a wonderful
legacy to leave behind.*

—Taylor Swift

Kindness, compassion, and respect go a long way (for a long time). The way we treat others often determines how people remember us. My principal emphasizes that the way a staff cares for its most vulnerable students defines a school's character. His mantra resonated with me strongly as a teacher, and it has improved my mindfulness of how I treat others on a daily basis. The reality is that kind people aren't always kind, and mean people aren't always mean, but everyone is something in each moment. If we become more mindful of the way we treat others in every situation, kindness will prevail, and people will prosper.

Unfortunately, school isn't always a kind place. Bullies can make life a living nightmare for others. In some cases, bullies don't understand the destruction of their words or actions. My heart aches for all victims of bullying, but it's hard to fault someone who honestly doesn't know the difference between what's right and what's wrong. That's why education is so important; it serves as a catalyst for enlightenment, acceptance, and maturity, which can reduce bullying incidents that are rooted in ignorance.

Other instances, where bullies are aware of their hurtful actions, are shameful. These incidents occur at alarming rates and are character crushers for both the victim and the bully. We are all different, but we all have weaknesses, we all have insecurities, and we've all made mistakes—we don't need others to magnify them for us (life is hard enough already). I could provide a specific example of bullying (sadly, I could give a hundred instances), but highlighting one situation would make it seem like it was worse than the rest. Whether you poke fun in person or behind someone's back, online or offline, or in seriousness or jest, preying on someone's mental, physical, social, or emotional vulnerability is never funny or cool.

Kindness is cool. **One act of kindness can be all it takes to make someone feel better about life.** It doesn't get much cooler than that. Opportunities to be kind or unkind will occur at school, and the way you act will create and reveal your character.

- If people are making fun of another student, will you join? Or will you demonstrate compassion and courage by standing up for that person?
- If the person in the cafeteria line is shy, will you jump the line in front of him? Or will you respectfully wait your

turn, even though you could save yourself some time at his expense?
- If someone embarrasses herself, will your actions make her feel worse or better?

Use these opportunities to lift others up by demonstrating empathy and integrity. Put yourself in the shoes of others, feel what they would feel, and act accordingly with kindness as your guiding light. Similar scenarios will continue to occur in different environments for the rest of your life, and you will notice that some people try getting ahead by belittling those around them. This shallow approach might even appear to work at first, but rarely does it pan out in the long run. Integrity and empathy come from the depths of your heart, so by exhibiting these qualities, you will never become a shallow person.

Remember that you cannot control how others act, but you can always control how you act toward others. Let your actions better the lives of those around you. When you view everyone as equal, every interaction will begin from a place of respect, but this can only occur if you first have self-respect. Holding yourself to the highest standards and instilling integrity in your life are sure ways to develop self-respect. Expect your best efforts and attitudes, and never diminish your self-worth. When you personally demonstrate high moral principles, you will create a culture of civility that endures throughout your life. Giving your best to others brings out the best in them. People will love being around you and will give their best back to you.

One last detail about respect: We often hear that it must be earned, meaning that you must first prove yourself to others before gaining their respect. While this is a common stance, it is equally important to understand that respect can also be learned. If you learn to begin each encounter from a place of respect, you will undoubtedly experience more civil and productive interactions. You'll be more open to new perspectives, your emotional intelligence will heighten, and you'll enjoy richer discussions. You will notice that you argue less, negotiate more, and become more concerned about what's fair and just. Through these adjustments, you'll earn the respect of those around you, which will bring peace and calmness into your life. When your head hits the pillow each night, you will fall asleep a little easier knowing you are a person who appreciates every life. And who doesn't love a good night's sleep?

Reflection and Self-Awareness Opportunity

1) Write down a time when you (or others) took advantage of someone.

2) Looking back, what could you learn from this experience? What could it teach you about respect? What could have been done differently?

3) Tomorrow, try to approach everyone you encounter from a place of respect. Write down what you notice.

7

Be a Goal Setter

As soon as I accomplish one thing, I just set a higher goal. That's how I've gotten to where I am.

—Beyoncé

In sports, scoring goals can make you a superstar. In life, setting goals can do the same. Successful people and goals go together like birthdays and cakes. Every year I meet students with big dreams, which is the way it should be, but it always concerns me how few students have set goals to help them achieve their dreams. Too many students simply hope that someday everything will work out for them. In life, greatness requires goals.

Goal setting aligns your realities of today with your dreams of tomorrow. It's smart to plan for your success. Peter Drucker popularized a simple SMART framework, which makes creating and achieving goals more manageable. **SMART** is an acronym that stands for **s**pecific, **m**easurable, **a**ttainable, **r**ealistic, and **t**ime bound. Formulating goals using this strategy allows you to start small while dreaming and achieving big. Being SMART about your goals is being smart about your life. For instance, the aspiration to "get in shape" is well intended but too vague, which makes it more of a hope than a goal. Using the SMART framework, you can better write this goal as "exercise for one hour, four days per week, for two months," thus changing a vague hope to get in shape into an achievable SMART goal with defined characteristics:

- It's *specific* because you lay out exactly what you plan to achieve.
- It's *measurable* because you can track whether you make it to the gym for one hour, four days per week.
- It's *attainable* and *realistic* because it's not suggesting you must work out for a crazy number of hours—only one hour per day, four days per week.
- And it's *time bound* because the two-month time frame keeps you motivated and accountable to stick to your plan.

Once you set your SMART goal, you must then consider what actions will help you achieve your goal. In this example, beneficial steps could be to create a workout plan, eat healthy foods, get proper rest, and convince a friend to join you on your fitness journey (developing a support network is always a good idea). Every goal needs an action plan. If you want to be an engineer, or own a car, or travel the world, think about immediate steps that could help you achieve your desires. Will you need a good education? Money saved? Communication skills? **Remember, your actions**

create your habits. When your actions become goal driven, achieving your goals will become a habit.

Although the future is unknown, you can still create a clear vision for yourself by having SMART goals fuel your actions. Just because you don't know what colors to paint the walls of a new house doesn't mean you can't start laying the foundation. SMART goals provide you with a stable structure on which to build your future. They sharpen your focus and help you become the person you dream of becoming. With properly set goals and a desire to develop, life will happen for you instead of happening to you. You'll go where you want to go, and you'll be happier because you brought yourself there. So much of school is performance based that it allows you multiple opportunities to set goals. These can relate to academics, sports, theater, personal development, or any curricular or extracurricular activity. If you start setting short-term goals now, you'll live an ambitious life filled with purposeful actions. That is one stellar combo.

Superstars are more than dreamers; they are doers. Walt Disney, an imaginative superstar who was once fired from a newspaper outlet for lacking creativity, believed that "all of our dreams can come true if we have the courage to pursue them." Whatever you are working toward, stick with it. Chase your dreams, but set SMART goals to make the chase easier. Write your goals down, and pin them up. Tell your friends about them, and establish a support network to help you along the way. Hold yourself accountable, and set expectations that promote development. Start small. Work hard. Achieve big. Then repeat. That's the evolution of a true superstar. Keep changing your world for the better. You've got this!

Even though this is the end of this chapter, I want to introduce three essential elements to also consider when achieving your goals: The importance of persistence—you must often endure the darkness of defeat before you enjoy the bright lights of success. The importance of sacrifice—achieving your biggest dreams will come at a cost. And the importance of happiness—you can't be so focused on future goals that you lose sight of your present joy. These traits are so important that they each have their own chapter.

Reflection and Self-Awareness Opportunity

Remember, be SMART when goal setting (specific, measurable, attainable, realistic, time bound).
   "**I will do better in school**" is better written as:
   "**I will improve my grades by 10 percent by the end of the school year.**"

Action plan:

- Ask more questions when I'm unsure of course concepts (support network).
- Study for tests without the distraction of my phone (sacrifice).
- Practice effective listening strategies from chapter 19 of this book (personal development).

1) **Start small:** Write down one short-term goal that you want to achieve within the next year.

Action plan: What strategies could help you achieve your goal?

2) **Dream BIG:** Write down one long-term goal (beyond one year from now).

Action plan: What could you do in the short term to help you achieve your long-term goal?

Stage 2
Develop Your Mind

The three great essentials to achieve anything worthwhile are, first, hard work; second, stick-to-it-iveness; third, common sense.

—Thomas Edison

If you want to create your best life, you must train your brain to accept challenges. This stage explores qualities that will strengthen your mind, improve your willpower, and help you achieve remarkable results in school and life.

8

Hone Your Work Ethic

What separates the talented individual from the successful one is a lot of hard work.

—STEPHEN KING

THE STUDENTS IN my tenth-grade literature class were always shocked when I told them that I did not care about their grades. It sounded odd, but it was true. I earned three university degrees and had various jobs and multiple interviews, and nobody ever asked about my tenth-grade literature mark (even when I was hired to teach the course!). It mattered that I had passing grades to move along in the education system, but whether I earned 60 percent or 90 percent or an A+ or C– did not matter. What mattered were my employability skills, which my work ethic helped develop.

The work ethic you display holds far more value than any grade you will ever receive. It is what's behind your grade that matters, so for it to have true meaning, you should follow this equation:

WORK ETHIC + ABILITY = YOUR GRADE

Consider the variables of this equation. While you might not fully control your cognitive abilities, you can always control your work ethic. Let me use two former students (and there are hundreds more just like them) as examples of why you should focus more on your work ethic than grades:

Jenna found schoolwork neither easy nor hard. She attended class, did her work, and put forth a decent effort that resulted in a grade of 80 percent. Because her mark was respectable, Jenna's parents and teachers were satisfied, so she was also OK with it. Deep down, however, Jenna knew that she coasted through the course activities and, as a result, experienced little development.

Erin, on the other hand, found schoolwork challenging but not impossible. She attended class, did her work, and put forth her best effort, which also resulted in a grade of 80 percent. Because she developed her work ethic and achieved a respectable mark, not only were Erin's teachers and parents pleased with her results, but Erin was also proud. Through determined efforts, Erin developed self-confidence and discovered problem-solving strategies that would help her in future learning environments.

Jenna's and Erin's identical grades of 80 percent suggest that they were on equal footing as students, but this is not the case. Your developments are direct results of your efforts, not your grades. Be honest with yourself, have high expectations, and celebrate a job well done. It's understandable that parents and teachers might be happy when your results meet their satisfaction levels, but that doesn't mean you should necessarily be satisfied. Only you truly know how hard you work and how much you challenge yourself to develop. You know when you can do more, and you also know when you do your best. So often in life, dedication dictates your destination.

Being naturally gifted is a welcome quality, but it can also prove detrimental if it decreases your motivation to push yourself. The problem with coasting is that it only takes you in one direction—downhill. Whenever you coast, like Jenna, opportunities to develop internally driven abilities that fuel a person's rise to success—such as self-discipline, resilience, or persistence—zoom past. You can acquire these valuable traits later, but you might have to learn a hard lesson first, since self-motivation, or lack thereof, is a habit that transfers to other areas of your life. A poor work ethic could cost you a job promotion, playing time on your team, or a starring role in the play. Skip the hard lesson by purposefully honing your work ethic.

When consistently giving your best effort—like Erin did—becomes a habit, you'll begin astonishing yourself and others. The hard work you do won't always be fun, but because you strive for greatness, you'll thrive in life. Legendary artist Michelangelo said, "If people knew how hard I work to gain my mastery, it wouldn't seem wonderful at all." Whether you are attempting to build skills or relationships, strive to become the Michelangelo of your class, your team, or your family by working your way to the results you want. Not only will you experience meaningful personal growth, but people will also love working with you as you lead by example. Remember that developing a strong work ethic takes purposeful actions over a sustained period. Humans are creatures and creators of habit, so be the hardest-working creature and create incredible habits. Giving your most genuine effort is a gratifying and inspiring way to live.

PS: Grades are valuable in many circumstances, but the need to attain specific marks for graduation, postsecondary acceptance, or scholarships still doesn't mean that's where you should direct your focus. If you concentrate on developing your work ethic, stronger academic results will inherently follow. And if you implement all of the advice from stage 1 of this book, receiving glowing reference letters from your teachers will be a breeze.

Reflection and Self-Awareness Opportunity

1) Think back to your previous year of school. Were you good at pushing yourself? Was your work ethic more like Jenna's (who coasted more often than she worked hard) or more like Erin's (who worked hard more often than she coasted)?

If you picked Jenna, what could you do to improve your work ethic? Try to be specific.

If you picked Erin, write down things you did well so you remember to keep them up!

2) Write about a time when you worked really hard to accomplish something. How did you feel afterward?

9

Develop Resilience Daily

It is not the strongest of species that survive, nor the most intelligent, but the ones most resilient and responsive to change.

—Charles Darwin

We live in a wonderful world, but it's not without problems and challenges beyond our control. Throughout life, you will face hardships that you cannot overcome or solve on your own—in such moments, be thankful for those who provide support and guidance. Some problems should not be tackled solo. But the truth is that in everyday life, what we sometimes consider a problem is more of an inconvenient change in our circumstances. Knowing how to take control of life's daily difficulties develops the responsive problem-solving power of resilience—a superstar quality that the world's most successful people possess.

Resiliency is your ability to recover from setbacks. For a variety of reasons, life often does not go as planned, so developing the willpower to bounce back from unfortunate changes strengthens your character and improves your life. School brings many opportunities to find solutions to everyday obstacles, yet every year I see capable students who struggle to take ownership of daily challenges. For instance, when essays are due in my classes, there are often students who will say, "Mr. Keliher, I don't have my essay because my printer broke," and then look at me as if this situation is no longer their concern but mine. The way you choose to deal with an inconvenience like a broken printer says a lot about your mindset and ability to overcome challenges.

Resilient people are problem solvers. You don't have to be an expert in printer repair to solve the issue of a broken printer. You could save your assignment to a jump drive. You don't have a jump drive? Borrow one from a friend. All your friends are asleep? Save your assignment online. Not tech savvy? Take pictures of your essay to show your teacher in the morning. No camera? Well, you might just have to go old school and write it out by hand (your grandparents would be proud). Always consider alternative solutions before giving up or offloading your inconveniences onto others. Although some solutions may initially seem more annoying than productive, champions see the value in doing the harder things in life. Writing an essay out by hand is not my idea of fun, but working through a setback (in this case to meet a deadline—an expected life skill) is a character-building quality that will serve you well for the rest of your life.

Resilient people are fighters from whom we can learn so much. Terry Fox. Helen Keller. If you don't know their stories, I urge you to look them up—both amazingly resilient leaders who inspired millions. Or how about professional surfer Bethany Hamilton? She lost her arm in a shark attack yet still returned to surfing, became a champion, and established a foundation that helps other shark-attack survivors and amputees. There is no denying that Bethany is an exceptional person, but if she can do what she did, then surely we can find ways to overcome life's minor setbacks. Imagine Bethany Hamilton as your teacher. Now imagine telling her that you gave up trying to find a way to print off your essay. Bethany may not be your teacher by title, but she delivers a tremendous lesson on how your mindset determines your ability to face challenges and contribute despite adversity.

Use your time in school as an opportunity to develop resiliency. Overcome your inconveniences by searching for solutions. Put in the extra focus and effort to get your work done well and on time. Find a tutor and try new strategies when learning gets tough. Ask questions when you need help. Don't have obstacles serve as excuses. **A resilient mindset, coupled with an internal work ethic and an external support network, will enable you to face any challenge with optimism.** Pushing through a setback builds grit, patience, and wisdom; you will rely on such traits for the rest of your days. As you grow up, troubles will arise, many of which will have higher stakes than a broken printer. Finding solutions to life's smaller challenges now better prepares you to conquer more significant setbacks that will inevitably come your way. With resiliency, instead of folding when times get tough, you will flourish.

Remember, while some challenges are merely inconveniences, others are much more significant. Life's hardest tests are best tackled with help from others, so tapping into support networks during these times is always the right thing to do. We all sometimes hide the battles we're fighting, but you'll encounter moments throughout your life when you need the support, guidance, and love of others. No one should walk in the dark alone. Human connection is essential for a healthy mind. If you are ever dealing with mental illness, distress, a low sense of self-worth, or extreme sadness or confusion in your life, it's imperative that you speak to someone. There will always be someone willing to listen and help. Also, you can contribute to your friends' resilience by checking in with them when you think they need support. Simply knowing, hearing, and seeing that others care about our well-being can provide us with the strength and courage to bounce back. Sometimes reaching out is the bravest, most resilient thing we can do.

Reflection and Self-Awareness Opportunity

1) List a recent setback that occurred in your life.

Circle the statement that best describes how you dealt with the situation:
    a) I was resilient. I used strategies to help me recover from my setback.
    b) I lacked resilience. I offloaded my problem onto someone else.
    c) I didn't do anything about my problem. I basically gave up.
    d) I tried to solve the problem on my own, but I should have sought support.

2) List a challenge where you needed to seek outside support. What was the benefit of using a support network?

3) Write down one person whom you trust to give you help and advice. Be sure to use this person when you need support or encouragement!

10

Discover the Importance of Persistence

After climbing a great hill, one only finds that there are many more hills to climb.

—Nelson Mandela

Persistence is a life-changing quality that allows you to battle through adversity and obstacles until you find success. It is similar to resilience in that both are internally driven but also complementary—where resiliency allows you to bounce back, persistence keeps pushing you forward.

Success is most rewarding when it is a culmination of hard work that has paid off over a series of trying times. In business, the path to success is often filled with potholes, detours, and roadblocks, so entrepreneurs who lack persistence typically don't last. They begin to doubt themselves, they lose motivation, and they eventually disappear. Legendary Apple Inc. innovator Steve Jobs said, "About half of what separates the successful entrepreneurs from the nonsuccessful ones is pure perseverance." It is often not a lack of intelligence or skill that holds us back but an unwillingness to embrace the daily struggles we face in our pursuit of success. Steve Jobs endured extremely tumultuous times and unsuccessful moments in his rise to superstardom, but his belief in himself and his vision for Apple products never wavered. He kept climbing hills. The results of his persistence include the formation of one of history's most creative companies and a legacy that will live forever. Persistence is key to growth and success, not just in business but also in school and life.

We are often told not to be afraid of failure, but this advice is only helpful if you possess the ambition to adapt when faced with difficulties. The late, great basketball coach John Wooden said, "Failure is not fatal, but failure to change might be." Without a willingness to make changes in our lives, outcomes will tend to stay the same. **Having the willpower to persist through challenging times develops flexible thinking skills that open your mind to new perspectives and solutions.** Let your challenges create positive change.

When you make purposeful adjustments after setbacks, failure becomes nothing to fear because it is no longer an endpoint. Like everyone who walks this earth, you will struggle in various areas of learning and life, but just because you grapple with something now doesn't mean it must remain a struggle forever. Your mind is a powerful tool, ready for development. The more you use your brain when challenged, the more it evolves. It's a lot like a muscle, and we know what happens when we challenge our muscles by exercising them. You have untapped skills that will reveal themselves if you have the patience and persistence to try new strategies in pursuit of solutions. In our world of instant gratification, patience and persistence are becoming endangered. To reach goals, build relationships, help others, and learn best, patience and persistence are paramount. Once these valuable qualities become habits of mind, you will become a mentally stronger person. Any failure that you endure will become just another step along your ever-changing path toward success.

School is a perfect environment to begin bursting through life's roadblocks. Unfortunately, too many students choose giving up instead of rising up during hard times. Throughout school, you will have courses, teachers, and projects that make your life difficult for a variety of reasons. Life might even seem unfair at times, but just because a class is complicated, a teacher is tough, or a project is a pain, don't relinquish your effort. Learning to persist through these turbulent times is one of the best lessons you can ever learn; it will prove more beneficial than any single course or assignment. Plus, if you persist, you'll more than likely conquer whatever poses the challenge or difficulty. It's a win-win.

Developing the habit of persistence now will help you deal with future challenges and setbacks. Occasions will arise when you feel like giving up. Other moments will occur when family, friends, and loved ones endure extreme hardships and want to crumble. Your ability to carry on can provide an encouraging attitude of strength, optimism, and hope that inspires others and makes pushing forward easier. Persistence is a life-changing habit and a fundamental ingredient of a superstar mindset. If you start developing it now, you'll rise to the occasion when you or others need it. Persistence brings achievement, inspiration, and admiration—all of which are superstar qualities. Never give up. Rise up. The view from the mountaintop is more magnificent when the climb is tough.

Reflection and Self-Awareness Opportunity

1) Overall, do you consider yourself a person who practices persistence?
           Yes   Sometimes   No

2) Write down a few tough situations that have occurred in your life (in or out of school) where showing persistence was needed.
   Situation 1:
   Situation 2:
   Situation 3:

3) Circle the answer that best describes how effective you were at showing persistence in each of the above situations.

Situation 1:	Situation 2:	Situation 3:
a) Very good	a) Very good	a) Very good
b) Good	b) Good	b) Good
c) So-so	c) So-so	c) So-so
d) Not good	d) Not good	d) Not good
e) Bad	e) Bad	e) Bad

4) How did you feel after the situation was over? Why did you feel the way you did?
   Situation 1:
   Situation 2:
   Situation 3:

11

Make Friends with Momentum

An object at rest stays at rest, and an object in motion stays in motion...

—Sir Isaac Newton

Beginning something is the first step toward achieving anything. Envision trying to roll out of your cozy bed on a cold morning. Hitting the snooze button while wrapped in warm blankets is a dream come true, and the thought of crawling out of bed is a nightmare, but once you are on your feet for a few minutes, starting your day becomes easy (most mornings). One reason that waking up can seem daunting some mornings is that you have yet to build any momentum in your day (all your energy is still under those comfy covers). Once you understand the power of generating consistent momentum for your actions, your daily decisions will make your life a dream come true.

To build momentum, you must first start something. I mean really start something. For example, some suggest that saving money for a new car is impossible without saving that first dollar. This advice, although painfully obvious, is valuable because saving your first dollar gets you started, which is important. However, with only one single dollar saved, you could likely spend your savings with little care—it was merely a dollar collected for a car that costs thousands. Having no momentum in pursuit of your goals makes maintaining motivation and dedication difficult. **Beginning something creates a beginner's mindset, but manufacturing momentum establishes a master's mindset.** If you save your first $100 instead of one dollar, then, all of a sudden, your mindset changes. You begin to envision yourself behind the steering wheel of your new car. With $100 saved, you are much more than started. You are on your way. You develop a savings mindset where contributing money to your car fund becomes a priority. Your $100 saved quickly becomes $200, then $600, then $1,600, and then, before you know it, *vroom*! Momentum gets you cruising in life.

Many students struggle in school because they never capitalize on the power of momentum. In the worst instances, students don't start anything, in which case there is little hope. In more common examples, however, students begin something, but their starts don't amount to much. They have a beginner's mindset. They pick up the pen but quickly put it down. They read the first chapter, then skip the next. They do a little bit of work here and put in minimal effort there. They go to school all week but stay home on Friday. They study for one test yet wing it on another. This "momentumless" lifestyle might be repeated for school years at a time! Many of these students have good intentions but never reap the benefits of momentum, thereby making achievement harder than it has to be.

Getting to a point where you benefit from momentum requires discipline and consistency. One of history's greatest thinkers, Aristotle, said, "We are what we repeatedly do. Excellence, then, is not an act, but a habit." For instance, studying for one test is good, but having the self-discipline to study for a few tests in a row makes studying a habit. Test preparation then becomes a natural behavior, and you learn more and perform better. Mastering one chord on a guitar is gratifying, but if you can master three chords through consistent practice, you are suddenly the life of the party. You will become eager to learn more chords and songs. Eating healthy and exercising for one day is smart, but keeping it up for two months will boost your energy and have you feeling awesome. Having the discipline to remain focused on your goals will create the consistent momentum needed to improve your productivity and results.

Use school to help you develop an unstoppable mindset that builds positive momentum. Whether it is in your class, in your band, with your sports team, or with your friends, commit to creating positive momentum in everything you do. Show up consistently. Work hard. Set SMART goals. Stay on track. And fight for results. Building positive momentum for yourself now will put you in motion for a life of success.

Note: Understand that momentum works both ways. It can accelerate your path to success or transport you to depths of despair. I have seen too many students gain such negative momentum that it transformed their lives in ways they would never have thought possible. Try to keep your momentum moving in a positive direction, but know that you will lose steam at times. Everyone does. When this happens, reflect, regroup, and refocus your priorities. Doing so will rebuild positive momentum. Generating momentum is easy when life is going well; it's when life is tough that positive momentum is harder to create, but the benefits of creating it are greater too. Resilience + persistence = positive momentum.

Reflection and Self-Awareness Opportunity

1) Describe a time when you built positive momentum in your life.

2) How did consistency or discipline help you build your positive momentum?

3) Describe an area in your life where you have struggled to build momentum.

4) What could you do to create momentum in this area?

12

Succeed through Sacrifice

The good and the great are only separated by their willingness to sacrifice.

—Kareem Abdul-Jabbar

You can do almost anything in this world, but you can't do everything, especially if you want to do things well. Your most ambitious achievements will often require great sacrifice. Every year I speak to students who have goals they wish to accomplish in school, music, sports, or other pursuits, which is exciting. Many of these students, however, aren't prepared to make the sacrifices necessary to fully achieve their desired results. Once you understand the importance of sacrifice, you will develop a powerfully ambitious mindset that helps you realize more of your goals. Sometimes you must give up a little to gain a lot.

Growing up, I had a best friend named Corey who, in eleventh grade, moved from our small town in Atlantic Canada to join a junior hockey team halfway across the country. Corey's decision to leave family and friends at only fifteen years old was tough, but he had a dream (a.k.a. long-term goal) of playing with the stars in the National Hockey League (NHL). Joining this team was a necessary step in pursuit of his goal. In his rookie season, Corey tallied only five points in fifty-seven games. That was hardly NHL material.

When his hockey season ended, Corey moved back home, and I was excited to pick up where we had left off as best friends. That summer, though, instead of hanging out like we used to, Corey was often busy training or going to bed early so he would be energized for practice the next day. These sacrifices were not easy for Corey, who loved to socialize, but becoming a professional hockey player was going to take hours of training, and he was motivated and willing to make the necessary sacrifices. The most rewarding sacrifices are often the hardest ones to make.

Teenagers today are busier than ever before, so developing the ability to prioritize will increase your willingness to make the sacrifices needed to achieve at your highest level. Prioritizing means examining your life's to-do list of wants and needs and determining their order of completion. Putting actions that most align with your values higher on your list makes sacrificing lower priorities easier. For example, if studying for a math test is high on your priority list because you value education, then an activity such as watching a movie, which might be more appealing at the time than studying math, becomes a more willing sacrifice. In Corey's case, his dream of playing in the NHL became his biggest priority, so he filled his life with actions that matched. Ensuring that your choices align with your goals will improve your decision-making and help you use your time meaningfully. We often want to try to do it all, but sticking to your priorities will always be worth it. Your life will follow a preferred path that you create, based on your deepest values and interests.

Think about your goals, and consider what sacrifices might help you achieve them. These sacrifices will differ in type and size. Whether it is forgoing junk food for healthier food choices, sacrificing new clothes for college savings, or passing on a party for piano practice, your willingness to sacrifice will help you realize what is truly important in your life. Sacrifice often separates the person who wants something to happen from the person who makes something happen. **In pursuit of a goal, sometimes what you don't do matters just as much as what you do, for it heightens your focus on what you value most.** If you learn to sacrifice today, you'll find yourself in a better place tomorrow. As my father used to tell me, short-term pain for long-term gain. Superstardom does not exist without sacrifice.

To this day Corey and I remain friends, but because of his desire to realize his goal, from that summer on, we didn't see each other as much. I did, however, see Corey one Saturday night on national TV, blasting his first NHL goal past legendary goaltender Martin Brodeur. It was inspiring watching him celebrate, knowing that it was a culmination of years of tremendous work and sacrifice. Corey made it!

While I reminisce about his success, I'm reminded of one more superstar quality that he displayed: modesty. This is something to remember as you find your own success. Even when Corey was playing alongside the world's best hockey players, he always remained humble. When we hung out, he was still the same Corey I had known since kindergarten. He was grateful for the support he received from family and friends. Corey made numerous sacrifices in order to find success, but one thing he never sacrificed was his personal character. Like I mentioned in chapter 6, the way we treat others determines how people remember us. I would never choose to share this story if Corey was a person of poor character. While the journey to the top is filled with sacrifice, never sacrifice your good nature; people will remember it above all else.

Reflection and Self-Awareness Opportunity

1) What are three current priorities when it comes to creating your preferred future? What could you sacrifice in order to achieve your goals?

   Examples:
   Priority: Write a song   Sacrifice: TV time
   Priority: Get along better with my sister   Sacrifice: Always getting my way

   Priority 1: _____
   Sacrifice(s): _____

   Priority 2: _____
   Sacrifice(s): _____

   Priority 3: _____
   Sacrifice(s): _____

13

Accept Challenges and Responsibilities

Laziness may appear attractive, but work gives satisfaction.

—Anne Frank

It may sound odd, but one of the best things to avoid in life is avoiding life. A life well lived is filled with responsibilities and challenges, and your willingness to accept these helps determine your integrity, growth, and impact. **Once you develop a mindset that values taking responsibility and tackling challenges, your life becomes more exciting and rewarding.** Superstars want the ball when the game is on the line.

When approached correctly, school and life should present challenging opportunities. Sometimes we rationalize avoiding responsibilities and challenges by convincing ourselves that what we are missing isn't a big deal. For instance, many students decide that the easiest way to deal with a difficult assignment is to simply not do it. I see this happen all too often. (I'm sure you can think of a classmate who fits this profile—hopefully it's not you, but if it is, thankfully you're reading this chapter!) Students avoid certain actions because completing them would create too much work or stress in an already hectic life. This thinking might be partially right—in the short run, you might prefer to skip an obligation rather than see it through—but developing the habit of avoidance when it comes to problems, challenges, or responsibilities will undoubtedly make your life more difficult in the long run.

Even if you can afford to take the easy way out at times, it doesn't mean you should. There are days when I'd rather stay home than go to work, but I still drag myself there; I have sick days that enable me to stay home, but I don't use them on these days because that's not their purpose. Doing so would be avoiding my responsibility, which is the wrong way to live. If I use my sick time for days when I just don't feel like working, I'll find myself in an unfortunate situation if I ever come down with an illness that keeps me bedridden for an extended period. Instead of avoiding it, I try to reframe my responsibility as an opportunity. On days where I am feeling unmotivated for work, I think about how grateful I am to have a rewarding job. Reframing a responsibility as an opportunity helps you see the positivity of any situation.

There is an expression that says, "Eighty percent of life is just showing up," and there is much truth to these words. Whether you face difficult days, challenging tests, or awkward conversations in the future, try to find the positivity and value in accepting responsibility, even if it seems painful at the time. Remember that you don't have to do everything alone. Use support networks, such as teachers, parents, or friends, when you need help, but always show up. Always do what's expected of you, and, better yet, go above and beyond expectations. You will become a reliable leader who is battle tested and willing to do what's necessary. People will admire your consistent approach to life. They will give you the ball when the game is on the line, and you'll be ready and willing to make the big shot. That sounds like superstar material to me. I can hear the crowd going wild!

Reflection and Self-Awareness Opportunity

1) Can you think of a time when you avoided responsibility? If so, what was it?

2) What could you have done differently?

3) What challenging times or big responsibilities are you approaching in life? How do you plan to deal with them? How could some of the qualities discussed in other chapters help you?

4) Describe a personal responsibility that is sometimes challenging to fulfill. How could you reframe this obligation as an opportunity?

14

Ignite Your Internal Motivation

I don't count my sit-ups. I only start counting when it starts hurting because then it really counts. That's what makes you a champion.

—MUHAMMAD ALI

Based on our discussion from the preceding chapter that "eighty percent of life is just showing up," then what makes up the other 20 percent? The answer is internal motivation. You see, doing something is all well and good, but doing something well is great. Once you become internally motivated to achieve in your daily pursuits, your potential becomes magical. Like a magician, you become capable of incredible results that others cannot imagine or replicate.

Internally driven people go beyond life's minimum requirements. In school, many students struggle to find the internal motivation to push themselves. Students often complete work but not to the best of their abilities. Countless people dedicate hundreds of hours to developing habits that promote mediocrity. Although doing something is better than doing nothing, it is still problematic. In the case of an assignment, it's not problematic because grades might suffer (remember, I care little about grades); it's problematic because settling for less than what you're capable of achieving is a bleak way to live. No matter what, minimum effort will never render maximum results.

Always strive for magnificence over mediocrity. External motivators, such as your parents, grades, or teachers, may spark your performance, but a spark can quickly fizzle out. When you learn to ignite the fire that exists within you, you develop a burning desire to succeed. You will become a person who accepts challenges, sees things through, and does things well. These behaviors separate the good from the great, the special from the spectacular, and the student from the superstar.

Once developed, internal motivation transfers to other areas of your life and propels you to future successes. You will begin succeeding not because other people want you to but because you demand the best that exists within yourself. School is the perfect opportunity to develop your internal motivation because of the broad range of courses you will take. Inevitably you will be expected to do things you like, things you dislike, and things you care little about. For the rest of your life, similar scenarios will occur, be it in your career, family, or other commitments. If you learn to treat all of these situations equally in finding the 20 percent needed to do all things well, your future self will thank you.

Tackling all challenges to the best of your ability now will prepare you to accomplish anything in the future. A life of high personal standards will become the norm.

Once internal motivation is part of your persona, you become someone who strives for success. You will develop the passion needed to embrace life's challenges. It is no coincidence that the most legendary names in music, sports, drama, and business hustled the hardest when no one was watching. **When practice is easy, improving is tough, but when practice is tough, improving is easy.** Superstars find the motivation within to put forth their best effort and to challenge themselves, no matter the circumstances. To quote the legendary boxer, Muhammad Ali, again: "I hated every minute of training, but I said, 'Don't quit. Suffer now and live the rest of your life as a champion.'" With internal motivation, you'll go the extra mile, and you'll be so happy and proud of your results that you wouldn't have it any other way. You will live your life like a champion. Ali would be proud.

Reflection and Self-Awareness Opportunity

1) Think about your previous school year. Which statement best reflects your current approach to schoolwork?
   a) When I have schoolwork, I try to find a way out of it.
   b) When I have schoolwork, I'm just happy to get it over with.
   c) When I have schoolwork, I put in effort, but I often know I could do better.
   d) When I have schoolwork, I am internally driven to do it well.

2) For what activity do you usually give your best effort?

3) For what activity do you typically lack the internal motivation to perform well?

4) What might be some benefits of performing both activities to the best of your ability?

Stage 3
Develop Your Opportunities

Opportunities multiply as they are seized.

—Sun Tzu

Opportunities exist all around you, every day, but you can only capitalize on them if you are aware of them. This stage focuses on recognizing opportunities that maximize your personal development and give each day more purpose.

15

Understand Opportunity Cost

*It is in your moments of decision that
your destiny is shaped.*

—Tony Robbins

Your decisions create your life. At some point, you've likely been told to weigh the pros and cons of each option when making a decision. That's solid advice to follow, but there is another useful decision-making strategy known as "opportunity cost." Essentially, opportunity cost means that once you make a decision, you have also decided to forgo all other possible options that you had. The unselected options represent the costs of your decision. Understanding this simple but powerful idea can help you make more thoughtful decisions and set you up for a better life.

Opportunity costs can take many forms. One that's easy to conceptualize is monetary. Anytime you spend the money you have, you then forgo your ability to pay for anything else with that money. Essentially, when you choose to buy something, you are deciding that you need or want that item more than anything else on earth at that time. It's an eye-opening concept when you consider past purchases. For instance, the opportunity cost of always spending your money on new clothing might be that you cannot save for college or a car. When you consider the opportunity costs of your financial decisions, you often become better at prioritizing your purchases, which results in you spending money more wisely and saving money more frequently.

Opportunity cost also exists in the form of time. Time is similar to money in that you should always be aware of how you spend it, but it's more valuable because the qualities you develop and memories you cherish over time are truly priceless. School provides you with precious time to learn, grow, and create memories. Learning in school extends far beyond course content; it exists in the opportunities you seize and the daily decisions you make. Many students limit their personal growth each day by not considering the opportunity costs of their decisions. For example, students skip classes for a variety of reasons. What they often do not realize is that the opportunity cost associated with skipping is much more than missing out on that day's lesson. If the only downside of skipping one class was missing course content, it wouldn't be a big deal (you could likely find the information online anyway). But when you analyze the act of skipping itself, especially when it becomes habitual, you begin to understand just how costly it is in terms of developing skills, abilities, and attitudes. Beyond missing the day's lesson, skipping class can result in decreased levels of work ethic, responsibility, persistence, and momentum. These developed qualities are pillars of success that you will need for the rest of your life, especially when life throws you a curveball. You cannot find these qualities online. You cannot acquire them by avoiding challenges. By skipping class, you forgo the development of valuable habits and replace them with habits of apathy and avoidance. That's a costly life decision. That's opportunity cost.

Making decisions based on opportunity cost requires maturity on your part because sometimes the decision you make after considering the opportunity cost might not be the most appealing decision in the short run. Here are a few examples:

1. **Decision:** Daydream in class
   Opportunity cost: Forgo learning new information and developing persistence
2. **Decision:** Eat the delicious, greasy meal that is calling your name
   Opportunity cost: Forgo the benefits of a healthier food choice
3. **Decision:** Stay up late to watch movies or play video games
   Opportunity cost: Forgo a restful sleep and a more productive tomorrow

While all three of these decisions might seem most enjoyable in the moment, understanding your opportunity costs allows you to weigh your options and make informed choices that align best with your values and goals. Whether it is the decision to buy clothes, sleep in, fake sick, succumb to peer pressure, or anything else, always try to consider what you're giving up when you make a decision—that's your opportunity cost.

The choices you make are ultimately up to you. Your daily decisions shape your future, so do your best to make intelligent choices while living a life you enjoy. There's still a time and place for staying up too late, eating greasy food, and even skipping class (that's right—I said it), but it takes maturity to understand when and how often to do these things. For every choice, there is an opportunity cost. **If you can save yourself from costly decisions, your time will be well spent, and your future will be rich.**

Reflection and Self-Awareness Opportunity

1) Think about an important decision you've made in the past year. What were some opportunity costs of that decision (i.e., what weren't you able to do as a result of your decision)?
Decision:
Opportunity costs:

2) After considering your opportunity costs, are you still happy with the decision you made?
Yes   No
If you answered no, why not?

3) Describe an upcoming decision you'll need to make. Remember to consider the opportunity costs of your choice before finalizing your decision.

16

Treasure Your Time

The most precious resource we all have is time.

—STEVE JOBS

TIME IS INCREDIBLY simple and profound all at once. It's simple in that we all get the same twenty-four hours in a day, yet it's profound because what we each produce with those hours creates our unique stories. Your life is precious, so you should treat your time as such. Learning to treasure your time will create a life filled with enriching experiences, golden opportunities, and priceless memories.

School is a perfect setting to witness time in action because students choose to use the same time so differently. There are many active learners who capitalize on numerous opportunities to grow both inside and outside the classroom. Watching these students make purposeful use of their time is uplifting. Unfortunately, there are also students who use their time in discouraging fashions. When students view school as merely somewhere they "have to go," they easily become disengaged. School is by no means a perfect place, and not every element of school will be your forte or favorite, but every minute you spend in school is part of your life story.

What you do with your time is what you do with your life. You won't always optimize your time, and that's OK, but be mindful of when those instances happen because awareness of how you use your time can reduce how often you misuse your time. When I was in tenth grade, my literature class began with twenty minutes of silent reading. I disliked reading, so I instead doodled the symbol of the iconic rap group Wu-Tang Clan and the Nike logo. Did my doodling skills help my future? No. Did I struggle with heavy reading assignments in university? Yes. Was doodling more fun for me at the time than reading? Absolutely. If I could go back in time, would I doodle again? Probably sometimes, but definitely not as frequently (remember, although I'm an optimist, I'm also a realist). I could not doodle my way through life and expect to see results. Life doesn't work that way. Actions that are repeated over time determine habits—and through my actions I developed the habit of being a distracted reader and avoiding challenges. It took me years of focused practice to improve my reading habits. My fifteen-year-old self would never have envisioned future me even reading a book, let alone writing one! If you spend enough time giving your best, you'll be amazed at what you can accomplish.

Your best habits create your best life. It's my sincere hope that your time in school is filled not only with learning and development but also with piles of smiles, laughter, jokes, fun, and friendship. Life should be joyful, so do your best to make it that way for yourself and others, but please understand that not every moment in your pursuit of joy must be enjoyable. Just because something isn't pleasant doesn't mean it isn't time well spent. Learning to struggle your way to success, while not always pleasant, is a tremendous use of time. Such experiences strengthen you, enlighten you, and eventually cultivate tremendous joy. If you want school to serve its full purpose, then you must embrace the times that are not conventionally fun. When you have difficulties with an assignment, a course, or a teacher, don't purposely zone out, give up, or settle for less than your best. Embrace these challenging times. Outside of school, put in the time to conquer the intricate guitar riffs, dance routines, or computational thinking skills. Leaning into challenging times is a superstar habit that leads to monumental breakthroughs, moments of excellence, and eventual joyous celebrations.

Every day you wake up, school day or not, cherish the time you have. It's an opportunity and a blessing. Make the most of your minutes because they create the hours that create the days of your life. Time truly is your most valuable resource. The time that passes will often exist in two forms. It will exist in a new version of you (for better or worse); time provides you the opportunity to develop skills, knowledge, relationships, and attributes that define you. Time will exist in memories, which are often up to us to create (keep that in mind the next time you play eight straight hours of video games or binge watch two entire seasons of your fourth-favorite show). Remember that others will also create their own memories of you, so spend time empowering those around you. Make people feel valued, loved, and respected. Show genuine interest in the lives of others. By treasuring time, you will accomplish and contribute more, create positive memories, and live joyfully, transformationally, and inspirationally. Go and have the time of your life.

Reflection and Self-Awareness Opportunity

1) Think about how effectively you use your time in school. Write down some ways you could make better use of your time.

2) Think about how effectively you use your time outside of school. Write down some ways you could make better use of your time.

3) Write about a time in your life that wasn't enjoyable (where you had to struggle) but, upon completion, brought you joy. Keep this experience in mind the next time you find yourself in a similar situation.

17

Make Room for Reading

A person who won't read has no advantage over one who can't read.

—Mark Twain

REGARDLESS OF YOUR post–high school plans, reading will be part of your life, so making it a priority now will only serve you well. Reading can inform, entertain, and change you in ways that other mediums cannot. **Simply put, deciding to read is deciding to grow.**

Too many students limit their development by limiting their reading. I've taught hundreds of students who, when asked what they read for fun, would reply that they never read for pleasure. They only read when something is assigned to them (and even then they might not read it). When you think about this, it's no wonder they dislike reading. If you only ever pick up a book after someone forces you, then reading and learning will only ever feel like a chore. Nobody likes chores.

Reading is exercise for the mind. It's a lot like running because it, too, can feel like a chore in the beginning. When you embark on your first run, your pace may be slow, and you may lack the stamina to run for an extended period before wanting or needing to stop. That's OK because everyone needs to find a manageable starting point. You may even dislike running initially (you certainly wouldn't be the only one), but with consistent practice and persistence, your speed and stamina will undoubtedly improve. Over time, positive momentum will build, and you'll impress yourself by running at faster paces for longer intervals. You might even begin to enjoy running so much that you become an avid runner. The same is true for reading. You may be slow initially and need to start with short intervals, but through persistent practice, you will improve your reading speed and stamina. Reading will soon become a natural, enjoyable activity. Eventually, you'll notice yourself reading for pleasure and getting better. Dedicated practice always leads to improved results.

Reading doesn't have to be a huge commitment. It can be fifteen minutes before bed, on the bus, or whenever and wherever. What you read can come from a variety of mediums like books, newspapers, or online sources. Just make sure that what you read has some substance. For instance, scrolling through social media or online shopping isn't focused reading, so it won't provide you with the same benefits as a book or article. Once you find the right material (it may take time, but you will), those fifteen minutes you allotted for reading will turn into hours where you are living inside the pages you read.

To make reading most enjoyable, read based on personal interests. If you choose what interests you, eventually the obligation to read will transform into an opportunity. Reading can provide an escape from reality, a time to unwind, or a challenge to the mind. Books can enhance your thinking by broadening your perspective. They can allow you to spend time with legends, from business icons like Steve Jobs or Oprah Winfrey, to beloved humanitarians like Princess Diana or Nelson Mandela, to celebrated superstars like Beyoncé or LeBron. So much can be learned from our world's most fascinating people, and books can offer a portal into their lives.

Once you become an avid reader, continue broadening your mind by sampling works of various authors, styles, genres, and cultures. Expand your horizons; there are phenomenal novels, biographies, memoirs, and other types of books filled with incredible ideas for you to explore. Oprah Winfrey emphasized the immense value of reading when she said, "Books were my pass to personal freedom. I learned to read at age three, and soon discovered that there was a whole world to conquer beyond our farm in Mississippi." And conquer she did. Reading can transform you by helping you see and understand the world and its possibilities from unimaginable perspectives. You will discover ideas that you never knew existed.

Reading is a healthy habit that will take you places, literally and figuratively. Carving out some regular reading time will make you more intelligent, imaginative, articulate, and open minded (pretty admirable qualities, if you ask me). Going forward, sacrifice some screen time, find a relaxing space, put down your phone, and pick up a book. And keep picking up books. Make reading part of your summer vacation; studies show that you'll be much better off when school starts up again. Also, without school obligations, summer is the perfect time to select your preferred choice of books.

By learning to embrace reading, you'll fill your mind with words of wisdom and make your own life's story even better.

PS: Thank you for reading this book. I know how precious your time is, and I appreciate your willingness to consider the thoughts within these pages.

Reflection and Self-Awareness Opportunity

1) Circle the statement that best applies to your current reading habits:
   a) I am an avid reader, and I read a broad selection of books.
   b) I am an avid reader, but I could broaden my selection of books.
   c) I read sometimes, and I'm eager to read more.
   d) I read sometimes but not as much as I should.
   e) I don't read as often as I should. I'm shocked I'm even reading this book!

   If you circled C, D, or E, what could you do to improve your reading lifestyle?

2) List some genres that you don't currently read but that might be of interest to you (e.g., nonfiction, fiction, biographies, history, war, graphic novels, poetry).

3) Write down two people you are interested in learning more about. Do an online search to find books written by them or about them.

18

Value Volunteerism

The best way to find yourself is to lose yourself in the service of others.

—MAHATMA GANDHI

THERE IS NO **bigger superstar than someone who helps others.** Life can be crazy busy, so it's admirable when people donate their own time for a cause they find worthy. Volunteers make society a better place. Think about your own life. It's likely that at some point you've been involved in a group or activity that was led by a volunteer. Maybe a special individual stands out as a role model or mentor. Valuing volunteerism is an easy way to improve your life while contributing meaningfully to your community.

We all have various life commitments, so it's easy to rationalize not having time to volunteer. You're correct in thinking that volunteering takes up time in an already busy life, but it can actually save you time by narrowing your interests, which can help you determine future pathways. I knew that I was interested in becoming a teacher, but after I volunteered at a camp filled with elementary schoolchildren, it didn't take me long to cross elementary school teacher off the list. Volunteering broadened my perspective yet narrowed my focus. Regardless of whether your volunteer experience is positive or negative, it will tell you something about yourself. Learning about you is always positive.

Many teenagers leave high school still unsure of their paths, which is normal, but this is often because some teenagers have yet to experience much for themselves. They've only done what they've had to do. Volunteering allows you to gain new experiences that can lead you down new roads and open up doors to places you'll love. Volunteering can help you find a passion for living and giving—a dynamic combination.

We live in a competitive world, and volunteering as a teenager can help you gain a slight edge over your competition in a job, college, or scholarship application. Volunteer experience shows that you are

- caring (you dedicate time to a cause that is important to you);
- hardworking (if you are willing to work for no money, imagine how hard you will work when you are getting paid); and
- mature (it is honorable to voluntarily serve others).

Employers and educational institutions love to see these traits in an application, and volunteerism demonstrates them brilliantly.

It's so important to help others, and what's neat is that when you help others, you also help yourself. When I reflect on the thousands of hours I have spent coaching, I feel happy and proud. I feel happy because it's something I enjoy—I've been places, developed relationships, learned a ton, and shared experiences that I'll remember forever. And I feel proud because I contributed to the betterment of others. Many coaches did the same for me when I was growing up, and I'm so grateful they did. It feels good to give back. Too often we get so caught up in receiving things that we forget the joy that giving brings. Helping others is always a worthwhile endeavor. Remember, the world needs you to care about it.

Volunteering doesn't have to be a big undertaking; in fact, you will probably want to start small. Your school community is a great place to begin because it will connect you to the school in a way that classwork cannot. When your school becomes a place to gain knowledge but also give back, your life as a student will have more purpose. Find a club or event that interests you, and see if you can contribute. It could be something that directly affects a small group of people in your school or something that raises awareness for a worthy cause in a different country. If you struggle to find anything of interest, gather some friends and create a volunteer group that matches your values. Everyone brings something unique to the table; do us all a favor by sharing your strengths and passions with the world in a way that helps others.

My only warning is that volunteering might lead you down unexpected paths, so be careful. Start volunteering, and the next thing you know, you'll be learning a whole lot about yourself, making new friends, gaining valuable experience, standing out among your competition, finding your passion, helping others, and feeling proud. That is a lot to have on your plate, but it's a pretty tasty dish, like my grandfather's spaghetti. I'd volunteer to eat that any day.

Reflection and Self-Awareness Opportunity

1) What is an activity/event you have done in the past that relied on volunteers? Do you think the volunteers were important? Why or why not?

2) For what type of activity/event do you think you might like to volunteer? What are some personal and societal benefits that could result from your contribution?

3) If you currently volunteer or have volunteered in the past, how did it make you feel?

19

Learn Effective Listening

When you talk, you are only repeating what you already know; but when you listen, you may learn something new.

—Dalai Lama

LIFE BECOMES BETTER when you are a competent communicator. Depending on your personality, your desire to speak in public settings may vary (although I encourage you to use your voice—too much excellent insight goes unheard in this world). Your decision to listen, however, has much less to do with your personality and more to do with your character. Effective listening involves being fully present in a given moment, which is a choice. **Your willingness to listen speaks volumes about your capacity to learn and contribute.**

Avid listening leads to avid learning; however, teachers often neglect to share advice about how to listen effectively. We readily mention tips for delivering a charismatic presentation, but when it comes to listening, you simply hear, "OK, class. Everyone, listen up!" Or the ever-so-detailed advice of "eyes and ears up here!" Listening is a skill we use every day, so it's worth knowing how to do it well.

The toughest part of effective listening is making the conscious effort to do so. School offers you opportunities to hone your listening skills in various settings with a variety of audiences. If you follow these three simple tips, you'll be set:

1. *Be an active listener.* Using nonverbal cues, such as nodding, smiling, laughing, or frowning, at appropriate times shows that you are engaged (doing these things at the wrong times can make for some awkward situations). Also, asking questions or clarifying points helps keeps you involved in the communication process. Active listening allows you to listen more closely. Make eye contact with the speaker (don't stare, though—that's just creepy), and have a posture that shows you are interested (even if you're not). When someone is speaking to you, don't slouch, put your head down, or lean way back in your chair. Being appropriately comfortable not only improves your alertness and ability to learn but also helps create a welcoming environment that puts the speaker at ease too. Plus, it's the respectful thing to do.

2. *Don't be thinking when you should be listening.* If a speaker makes a point that you disagree with or that you would like to comment on, don't immediately start planning a rebuttal or comment in your head. When you start thinking, you stop listening and could miss the rest of the speaker's point. Listen to understand. Always hear the speaker's complete message before turning attention to your thoughts. You will get your chance to talk, and by

listening for the entire time, you'll have more information to draw from when forming your points.

3. *Take notes* (when necessary or appropriate). If you use this tip on a first date, it will likely also be your last date with that person. If you use this tip in class, it can be a big help. Jotting down a speaker's key points can help you retain information. It can also keep you on task and help you refrain from overthinking when you should be listening. Then, when it's time to speak, you can refer to your notes to help gather your thoughts. Instead of trying to remember key points, you'll have valuable information written down that you can review. Plus, if you plan to attend postsecondary school, notetaking will be expected, so you might as well begin practicing now.

You'll notice from these tips that effective listening involves more than just your ears; it's about being fully present in a given moment, which is such a superstar quality. School provides many academic and social opportunities to develop your listening skills, so make your time meaningful. Although effective listening traits are not complicated, they require character, discipline, and enthusiasm; these qualities enable you to actively contribute to a conversation even when it is not you doing the talking. Through active listening, you'll create an environment where those who are speaking feel valued, which will help them communicate best. You will absorb new information and enjoy more enriching dialogue. By learning to listen, you'll turn your life up a notch.

Reflection and Self-Awareness Opportunity

1) Rate yourself out of 5 for the following statements.
   Legend: 1 = Never   2 = Rarely   3 = Sometimes
           4 = Often   5 = Always
   I make appropriate eye contact when someone is speaking to me in a group setting.
   1   2   3   4   5
   My posture conveys that I am an engaged listener.
   1   2   3   4   5
   I use nonverbal cues (nodding, smiling, etc.) to show that I am an active listener.
   1   2   3   4   5
   I listen until the speaker is finished before I begin constructing my thoughts.
   1   2   3   4   5
   When appropriate, I jot down key points that a speaker mentions.
   1   2   3   4   5

2) Try to employ the chapter tips about effective listening during your next class. Write about what you noticed afterward.

20

Step Out of Your Comfort Zone

The biggest risk is not taking any risk…in a world that is changing so quickly, the only strategy that is guaranteed to fail is not taking risks.

—MARK ZUCKERBERG

IF LIFE WERE filled with doors of opportunity, everyone would walk on through to success. But life is not that easy. Instead, the saying we use is "a window of opportunity"; to capitalize, you must be willing to get uncomfortable and climb through. Life experiences that bring the best opportunities and rewards are often those in which we must step out of our respective comfort zones. Voluntarily taking some personal risks is a courageous act that pushes boundaries, fosters development, and drives success.

School is supposed to challenge you, but sometimes it is up to you to create the challenge. For instance, high school provides you with opportunities to enroll in subjects or programs about which you might know little or nothing. Don't immediately dismiss these options. Too many students opt for courses in their comfort zones instead of using the opportunity to expand their horizons. I, regretfully, was one of those students. My high school offered culinary and carpentry courses, but I opted for physical education courses, which were more in my comfort zone. I was already exceptionally active outside of school, so I didn't need the daily physical activity in school, but I knew I'd find the courses comfortable. Now, at age thirty-two, I'm still physically active (I would be regardless of whether or not I took phys ed courses), but my culinary and carpentry skills remain minimal. Instead of taking a personal challenge in school, I settled for comfort and missed an opportunity to develop. I won't go so far as to say I made the wrong choice by taking phys ed instead of other courses (there's value in following your interests and passions), but I didn't give those options the consideration I should have. Who knows—maybe I would have become a world-famous chef! Hors d'oeuvres, anyone?

Many opportunities for taking personal risks exist in school, so dare to explore beyond the classroom. Famed explorer Christopher Columbus said, "You can never cross the ocean unless you have the courage to lose sight of the shore." Believe in your ability to tread in unknown waters and face new challenges. These actions often lead to life-changing discoveries. Explore your creative side, and share your ideas with others. Audition for the play, and try out for the team. Ask that special someone on a date (you know whom I'm talking about). Start up a business or a band. Make new friends, and try new foods. Challenge your work ethic, and embrace the unknown. You'll never know the amazing things you can do until you try doing amazing things.

The more you step into unfamiliar territory, the more you will learn and the braver you will become. Stepping out of your comfort zone may cause some stress, but this stress, in moderation, is healthy, as it leads to personal growth. Although taking a personal risk might be scary initially, what's neat is that the more you do it, the easier it becomes. Your comfort zone expands every time you challenge yourself, which is helpful because life will challenge you. You will find yourself in future situations (often unwillingly) where you feel uncomfortable, anxious, or insecure. Voluntarily living bits of your life outside your comfort zone now will improve your ability to handle the unexpected trials that will inevitably come your way. The bottom line is that life's epic moments rarely occur inside comfort zones. **Unfamiliar territories and uncomfortable challenges create unforgettable experiences and unprecedented growth.**

Just remember that too much of anything is detrimental, including taking on too many challenging endeavors at once. Don't push yourself too far too often. First, take smart risks only—never jeopardize your safety or your future by taking unsafe risks. Your life is too valuable. Second, balance is key. Sometimes staying in your comfort zone is the best move. For instance, if you already have a challenging course load, then choosing a less challenging elective might be the right decision. Find a healthy balance in everything you do, but remember that being comfortably uncomfortable is a healthy way to live; that's when you're really in the zone.

Reflection and Self-Awareness Opportunity

1) How often do you step out of your comfort zone?
   a) I never step out of my comfort zone.
   b) I rarely step out of my comfort zone.
   c) I sometimes step out of my comfort zone.
   d) I often step out of my comfort zone.
   e) I step out of my comfort zone whenever I get the chance.

2) Write down an opportunity you have to step out of your comfort zone. What might be some potential benefits of this experience?

21

Never Stop Learning

Once you stop learning, you start dying.

—Albert Einstein

From her nursing home, my eighty-seven-year-old grandmother continued to model the advice she gave me when I began my teaching career. A retired teacher herself, she was adamant that even though my job was now to teach others, it was imperative that I never stop learning. My nannie's physical health was in decline, but her mind was vibrant. She read widely, she listened and asked questions during our conversations, and she tackled new challenges every day. She was still learning, and it was inspiring. Lifelong learning is vital to personal growth and a life well lived.

To live a life where learning is continuous, you must be teachable. Once you develop teachable characteristics, your acquisition of knowledge will never stop, and you augment your ability to contribute. Teachable people share the following four traits:

They accept that learning is a challenge. Wanting to know what you don't yet know is a challenging opportunity. For some students, unknown possibilities can frustrate and freeze learning, but for teachable individuals, these same unknowns fuel learning. If you view learning as a challenge, you become more prone to doing what it takes to learn. Instead of crumbling when learning gets tough, you will have the work ethic, inquisitiveness, and persistence necessary to succeed. Superstar artist Pablo Picasso said, "I'm always doing that which I cannot do, in order that I may learn how to do it." Challenging yourself to learn will broaden your repertoire of skills. Knowledge is power.

They are optimistic about learning. Teachable people recognize that learning can happen anytime, anywhere, from anyone. For a variety of unfortunate reasons, many students bring pessimistic attitudes into the classroom. You might believe you have good reasons for such a stance, and who am I to tell you that you're wrong? Heck, you might be right; people often come from challenging circumstances that are beyond their control. But remember that the attitude you bring into any environment is a personal choice you make each day. **It is the mindset, not the mind, that fuels our learning and growth.** Many students stand on similar footing from an intellectual standpoint, yet the amount they learn in classes varies tremendously. Choosing a positive attitude that views each day as an opportunity to learn will enrich your educational experiences and make your life more fulfilling.

They never give up. For teachable people, failure is part of their learning process; it's sometimes necessary but always temporary.

When you can accept disappointment and criticism yet push forward, you learn. When you can own your mistakes and keep going, you learn. When you can look yourself in the mirror and know that you are capable of changing, even though it may be difficult, you learn. Teachable people never give up; in fact, it's often during tough times that they learn the most.

They are critical thinkers. Teachable people possess curiosity, which evokes a willingness to unpack new ideas and concepts through the use of various strategies. They are open to asking questions, considering alternate viewpoints, seeking out new information, engaging in dialogue, and evaluating sources before passing honest judgment. Martin Luther King Jr. believed that "the function of education is to teach one to think intensively and to think critically." Critical thinkers are continuously evolving, so they feel comfortable accepting constructive feedback, changing their opinions, and admitting when they are wrong. While some people believe that such qualities are signs of weakness, they are actually signs of wisdom. By developing a desire to think critically, you'll become a more informed and compassionate person. Such people tend to listen, read, and think more before they speak, write, and act, which are definitely behaviors worth learning.

Education extends far beyond the walls of a classroom. It exists on the fields and courts. At the musician's and painter's studio. In the pages you read and the shows you watch. During times of love or heartbreak, joy or suffering, life will never stop presenting learning opportunities that foster growth. Some will be easy to recognize in the moment (open your math book to page 223) and others more veiled (the death of a loved one might teach you to cherish your life and relationships more closely). Learning will happen all around you for the rest of your days. It is said that with age comes wisdom, but this is only true if you are willing to process learning opportunities over time.

The more teachable characteristics you possess, the wiser you will become. With my grandmother on my mind, I'm reminded that we can gain so much insight from our elders. Older people have invaluable knowledge and life experiences—they've learned, experienced successes, and made mistakes. Spend some time with them, ask them questions, and embrace the opportunities to learn from the people who came before us. They often love to share their insight with the younger generation. Plus, you and I will be them someday, if we're lucky. I'm sure we will appreciate the conversations and company too.

One more side note about my nannie—she passed away shortly after I had written this chapter. I was fortunate enough to spend her last few days by her side. She was a widow who lived in a nursing home, and up until the moment she died, she was still as loving, kind, and grateful as ever. Her endearing qualities will live on through the people she profoundly influenced during her life. She taught me that when such qualities are part of your character, they never leave. That's a lesson worth learning. Superstars are truly everywhere.

Reflection and Self-Awareness Opportunity

1) Rate yourself out of 5 for the following statements to evaluate your teachable characteristics.
   Legend: 1 = Never   2 = Rarely   3 = Sometimes
              4 = Often   5 = Always

   a) I rise to challenges that are placed before me.
      1   2   3   4   5

   b) I view an experience as an opportunity to learn.
      1   2   3   4   5

   c) I view failure as an opportunity to come back stronger.
      1   2   3   4   5

   d) I use critical thinking strategies to better inform myself.
      1   2   3   4   5

2) Circle the teachable characteristic that you could improve upon the most:
   a) Accepting that learning is a challenge
   b) Being optimistic about learning
   c) Never giving up
   d) Thinking critically about ideas

Stage 4
Develop Your Leadership

Change will not come if we wait for some other person or some other time. We are the ones we've been waiting for. We are the change that we seek.

—Barack Obama

Positive change is impossible without an internal desire to improve. This stage focuses on developing leadership characteristics that allow you to serve yourself and others best.

22

Believe in Yourself

The first step is you have to say that you can.

—WILL SMITH

IT IS INCREDIBLE how much potential and opportunity you have at your age. For instance, right now there are future prime ministers or presidents, groundbreaking scientists, and world-class musicians who are roughly your age. I hope they are reading this book (that would be cool). You might be one (that would be cooler). It's neat to think about that stuff, and I hope you do think about that stuff. Your future is unwritten, but you are the author. Do your best to write an epic life story. To fulfill your dreams, it's imperative that you believe in yourself. How much you believe can determine how much you achieve.

Sometimes life is all about confidence. In my classes, many students despise delivering presentations because they're nervous about what their peers will think. Public speaking is a real fear for many. I remember one student, Nate, who delivered a presentation in my class, and in all honesty, it was horrendous. He hadn't rehearsed, he looked nervous, and he spoke quietly and cautiously. He did pretty much everything you're not supposed to do when presenting. His performance wasn't entirely shocking, though, because Nate had become accustomed to failing assignments over the years. When it came to schoolwork, he had zero confidence. With no confidence, he lacked the ambition needed to improve.

After his presentation, I asked him how he thought it went. His response was, "Not good. I suck at presenting." The first part of his analysis was true—his presentation was far from good. The second part, however, was where the real problem existed. "I suck at presenting" really meant "I don't believe in myself."

You will struggle with any act when you don't believe in yourself. It's good to be self-aware and realistic about your flaws, but be careful that you don't sell yourself short. We all have weaknesses, but that doesn't mean they can't one day be strengths. We all have doubts, but that doesn't mean they can't one day be beliefs. We all have dreams, but that doesn't mean they can't one day be realities. Sometimes the real reason we're unsuccessful is that we lack the confidence to succeed.

I knew Nate was capable of better work than what he had produced because I had witnessed him interact with classmates. He was funny, engaging, and outgoing—all elements of a talented presenter—so I wasn't buying his story that he "sucked at presenting." When I pointed out Nate's strengths to him, he reluctantly agreed with me but also sheepishly smiled. By realizing his capabilities, I watched his mindset change from "I suck at everything I do in school" to "I have skills and talents." He was developing self-confidence, which is a vital ingredient to self-improvement.

With his next presentation, Nate shocked the class. He was the same person physically; he wasn't any smarter than before, but the way he believed in himself transformed his entire demeanor and showcased his strengths. His presentation was so impressive (and so shocking) that he received a standing ovation from his classmates. He inspired those lucky enough to witness this tremendous act of personal leadership, and his success at that moment spread confidence into other parts of his life. He improved his work ethic, became more responsible, and was a happier individual—all because he believed in himself.

Whether it is school, music, sports, or anything else, never diminish your self-worth. Self-confidence improves your mindset, which helps you find the qualities needed to overcome obstacles, face fears, step out of your comfort zone, and shock the world. Get to know your inner superstar. Celebrate your strengths, and work on your weaknesses. View disappointments as character builders, and come back stronger. Surround yourself with people who motivate you and believe in you. Be someone who believes in others. And on days when you're lacking self-confidence and feel as if no one believes in you, please remember that I do (I wouldn't have written this book if I didn't). It's always good to have a fan club.

Note: Be careful not to confuse the beneficial quality of confidence with the destructive attitude of arrogance. The great philosopher Lao Tzu suggested that "if you want to lead them, you must place yourself behind them." Arrogance places you ahead of others (often in your eyes only), which then diminishes your ability to lead and contribute. The encouragement you give others will come back to you and help fuel your own self-confidence. Everyone's performance elevates when they feel supported. **Believing in yourself and others will make your life unbelievable.**

Reflection and Self-Awareness Opportunity

1) Write down two of your best qualities that allow you to contribute at a high level. Remember not to sell yourself short. You are a superstar!

2) In BIG PRINT, write something that you'd love to accomplish. Remember to dream big. If you believe it, you can achieve it.

3) How could you show someone close to you that you believe in him or her?

23

Don't Let Your Past Define You

*I've failed over and over and over again in my life…
and that is why I succeed.*

—Michael Jordan

Sometimes there's nothing better than a fresh start. In my school, student grades range from tenth through twelfth, and although I teach all grades, my favorite classes are first-semester tenth-grade classes because it's a new school year, a new environment, and a new life chapter for students. But although everyone has a fresh start, it doesn't mean everyone starts fresh. Some people let their pasts limit their futures. **Don't let your yesterdays ruin your todays and restrict your tomorrows.** Every day can serve as a new beginning for your life's path because it is an opportunity for change, growth, and greatness.

Even when we're given a new opportunity, it's understandable why we might fill a clean slate with negativity right off the bat. We often derive negativity from unfavorable past experiences (history does have a way of repeating itself). For instance, if you struggled with various aspects of school in the past, assuming that these negative experiences will continue in the coming school year might be logical. While this thinking is understandable, it doesn't mean it's the right mindset. Living in the past makes it difficult to move forward. Why let your thoughts limit your potential? It's true that your prior experiences have shaped who you are today, so it's important to acknowledge the past, but your past does not define who you can become. Part of your personal growth is adapting and, in some instances, reinventing yourself.

The world's most successful people use their pasts as building blocks instead of roadblocks. Superstar athlete Michael Jordan, arguably the greatest basketball player of all time, was cut from his high school varsity basketball team. If he had labelled himself as a second-tier athlete after being cut, he would've never worked on his skills enough to become the sports legend he is today (and I would've never had the coolest sneakers in fourth grade). Another example is famous author J. K. Rowling. Numerous publishers initially rejected her story of Harry Potter, which would become one of the most popular book series of all time. If she had let those rejections define her as an author, she would've never found the resilience and persistence to bring her international bestselling novel series to fruition (and I would've never learned the meaning of a muggle). In both cases, their pasts didn't define who they were. Instead, their backstories helped create whom they would become.

It's difficult to fathom the past struggles of superstars like MJ and JK given their iconic successes, but their stories highlight how legends are made and not born. Michael Jordan or J. K. Rowling were once teenagers just like you. You, too, can become a superstar in life. You can be the best version of yourself, and for that, there are no comparisons. Your success truly knows no boundaries.

Every day provides an opportunity to redefine your life. Just because you were a bad student (or friend, or anything else) last year, last week, or even today doesn't mean you must label yourself as such moving forward. Instead of focusing on your past, envision the person you'd like to be in the future, and use this vision to guide your present actions. Doing so will give you a renewed sense of purpose and drive, which will help you achieve your goals.

Remember, changing your outlook on life can change your life. On the flip side, if you have done well in the past, it doesn't mean you'll continue to do well without putting in the focused effort. The future allows for improvement and decline—which one occurs is often up to you. And although your past cannot define your future, certain consequences of past actions can limit future opportunities, so always be aware of the decisions you make and the potential consequences of your choices. Not letting your past define you is a wonderful present to give your future. (See what I did there? Past, present, future? Well, I'm impressed, anyway.) Becoming legendary begins today.

Reflection and Self-Awareness Opportunity

1) What is something from your past that you feel defined you in a negative way? Is that how you define yourself today? If so, how would you prefer to define yourself?

2) What daily actions could help you reinvent yourself and focus on your present opportunities instead of your past?

24

Be Better Than You Were Yesterday

The day you think there are no improvements to be made is a sad day for anyone.

—Lionel Messi

A friend of mine shared a picture online of a whiteboard that hung in her fourteen-year-old son's room. On this board he had written the quote, "The only person you should try to be better than is the person you were yesterday." I had heard or read this expression many times throughout my life to the point where it seemed cliché, but when I processed that this teenager had purposefully put it on his whiteboard, it suddenly connected with me. I thought, If this fourteen-year-old actually commits to living by this quote, he is going to lead one phenomenal life.

Your teenage years are transformative times when your daily actions are critical to your development and identity. Seeing students develop from timid teenagers into confident young adults ready to take on the world is the uplifting, sunny side of student transformation. Unfortunately, there is also a heartbreaking, darker side. Every year, teenagers with a world of potential go from having so much promise to so little hope. Students often don't realize that their daily decisions are creating their negative transformation. Their downward spirals, whether because of social issues, personal issues, drug issues, or any other reason, often begin with small daily actions that snowball exponentially over time. By taking time to evaluate your life and its path on a daily basis, you can help ensure that you are living a life you love.

Trying to be better than you were yesterday speaks of gradual improvement. The truth is, life will not always feel like constant improvement. You (and everyone else on earth) will endure bad days when you do and say things you regret, use poor judgment, and more. Obviously, you want to limit these days, but they are inevitable. So, more specifically, you want to avoid having a number of these days consecutively. By asking yourself the question, "Am I a better person than I was yesterday?" you can limit your potential losing streaks and prolong your winning streaks. **Gradual improvement is key; with enough daily wins, you become an all-star.**

There are different ways to approach the question, "Am I a better person than I was yesterday?" You can assess your overall self in a general sense (am I a better person?), or you can break down your gradual transformation into the various components of your life (are you a better son or daughter, brother or sister, friend, student, teammate, band member, role model, etc.?). You can also focus on personal traits as a way to assess your gradual transformation (are you more patient, social, disciplined, positive, better at listening, etc.?). A daily checkup will keep you on track and provoke personal changes that also positively affect those around you.

Trying only to be better than yourself also keeps you from unneeded comparisons to others. School can become a hot zone for comparing grades, social status, talents, looks, or anything else. These comparisons are sometimes helpful and healthy when they serve as motivators, but too often they are physically, mentally, and emotionally draining. You can take control of your future and your well-being by focusing on what you can control—your own life. We are now so frequently inundated with filtered, edited highlights of other people's lives that it can hinder our ability to appreciate our own. We often choose to compare in terms of what we don't have. We look at others and fill our minds with what we perceive to be wrong or missing in our lives. We generate self-pity and a negative attitude instead of self-assessment and genuine gratitude. The latter two are so much more beneficial, for they allow us to reflect and realize how fortunate, gifted, and blessed we are in so many ways.

Whether you get every break in the world or you have all odds stacked against you, it is always up to you to make the most of your life. A life well lived is composed of worthwhile daily actions. You deserve your best attitude and effort. Your life is what you make of it, so why not try to make it better every day? If you do, you'll lead an amazing life, one day at a time.

Reflection and Self-Awareness Opportunity

1) Write down two ways that you could become a better person than you were yesterday (or in the recent past). Explain what daily actions you would take in order to improve.

1.

Actions:

2.

Actions:

2) Write down a time when you negatively compared yourself to others. How did it make you feel? What could you have done instead?

25

"Don't Worry, Be Happy"

There is no path to happiness; happiness is the path.

—Buddha

Happiness is one of life's finest feelings, yet too often we do not let it into our lives. My brother used to quote the title of Bobby McFerrin's famous song "Don't Worry, Be Happy" at the end of every email he sent. One day I asked him why he selected that quote, and he said, "Everyone can understand it, everyone can put it into practice, and it's a good general mantra." I loved his answer. Our mindset controls our willingness to be happy. Choosing to live a happy life will lead you down a path of positivity, making every day more remarkable.

Let's get this straight: focusing on happiness does not mean that you will always be happy, but it means that you will likely be happy more. Your worry and your joy, along with a host of other feelings, are generated from within your mind and heart. "Don't worry, be happy" acknowledges that tough times exist in life (the "don't worry" part), but it also emphasizes how you control the way in which negative experiences affect you (the "be happy" part). Consciously deciding to focus on the good that exists in your life inherently makes it easier to deal with the bad.

We often become so stressed that we forget about happiness. There is no denying that school, and your teenage years in general, brings stressful and anxious times (a.k.a. worry). You have plenty to consider, ranging from social situations and financial issues to academic expectations and future considerations. Stressful events are going to continue to exist for your entire life, just in different ways. In knowing that, it's important not to let these worries dominate your thoughts and bring you down. I'm not suggesting that you should avoid responsibility; instead, adopt a mindset that accepts life's realities and deliberately focuses on the positives of any situation. Your mindset plays a key role in establishing your mood. For instance, school isn't always the most fun place, but instead of viewing school as somewhere you have to go (negative outlook), see it as a place you get to go (positive outlook)—formal education is a privilege that millions of teenagers around the world do not get to experience. If you dislike a course, focus on the opportunity to be with your friends, or practice patience and persistence. When friends aren't in your class, focus on the chance to step out of your comfort zone and make new friends. A shift in your perspective can be all it takes to turn obstacles into opportunities and unhappiness into happiness.

Choosing to focus on the positives will improve your life in more ways than you realize. Oscar Wilde said that "to live is the rarest thing in the world. Most people just exist. That is all." With a mind and a heart that seeks happiness, you will feel more alive, which is the greatest feeling that we so naturally take for granted. You'll laugh and smile more. You'll do more of what you love. You'll see more value and meaning in every experience. You'll give more to others and forgive more easily. You'll develop closer relationships and bounce back more quickly. You'll be proud of yourself and celebrate the success of others. You'll be more calm and compassionate. You'll become a grateful person who feels less stressed and more blessed. What's neat is that all these benefits of happiness also bring more happiness, so the effects of positive thinking will multiply to create an increasingly enriching life of abundance. **A plant still grows in rain, but a ray of sunshine makes a world of difference; positivity will only help you blossom into a beautiful person who leads and loves.**

Remember, happiness is a perspective. Spend time doing what makes you happy, but know that with the right mindset, you can always make happiness a reality. At times, life will still be unfair, no fun, and downright cruel, but living by the simple mantra "Don't worry, be happy" will shift your focus from negative to positive, no matter what life throws at you. Bad days are part of a good life. They allow you to come back stronger and wiser. With a positive attitude, the happy moments in life will become more enjoyable. The bad moments will still happen; they just won't seem as bad. And that's good. That's something to be happy about. I'm doing my happy dance right now.

Reflection and Self-Awareness Opportunity

1) **Don't worry:** In general, how much time do you spend worrying about things you can't control?
   a) I spend way too much time worrying about everything.
   b) Even though I try not to, I often find myself worrying.
   c) I typically don't worry about things I can't control.

2) **Be happy**: In general, how happy are you?
   a) I am generally an unhappy person.
   b) I am up and down when it comes to happiness.
   c) I am generally a happy person.

3) Write down three things in your life for which you are grateful.

   1.

   2.

   3.

Smile! That list is something to be happy about.

4) Now shift your focus. Write down one thing that would typically make you unhappy, and try to find the positive that exists in it.

Example:
Negative: Got into an argument with my close friend

Positive: Had the chance to discuss the problem together and make our friendship stronger

Negative:

Positive:

26

Be True to You

Today you are you. That is truer than true. There is no one alive who is youer than you.

—Dr. Seuss

Only those who remain true to themselves live their finest life. Being yourself is not always easy, but it is essential if you want to perform at your highest levels. The sooner you realize how special you are and how much control you have in your life, the sooner you'll be able to appreciate your unique awesomeness and share your best self with the world.

You cannot be yourself when living in the minds of others. Too often we become concerned with what someone might think of our personality, style, or abilities that we start making decisions based on others' thoughts instead of our own. These concerns breed anxiety, which creates unhealthy stress, doubt, and insecurity in our lives. Negative thoughts can alter our behaviors and moods and make us act in unauthentic ways. It will serve you well in school and throughout your life to worry less about fitting in and more about standing out. We are all different, and that's what makes us special. Superstar musician John Lennon explained it in simple terms when he said, "It's not weird to be weird," so celebrate your weird self. The Leaning Tower of Pisa is a beloved landmark because it is crooked; embrace what makes you different. *Unleash your quirky personality*—it's a rare gift. *Showcase your strengths*—they allow you to serve yourself and others best. *Acknowledge your weaknesses*—they can transform into strengths only once identified. You are a one-of-a-kind, extraordinary gem. **Having the courage to be the most positive, authentic, and ever-improving version of yourself is the most precious gift you can give the world.** There truly is no one else in the world like you.

You cannot be true to yourself if you say one thing but do another. Making intentional choices that reflect your values is essential for a life well lived. While this idea sounds straightforward, it is often poorly executed. For instance, some people claim to value kindness, yet their actions belittle others. Some claim to value education, yet they do not challenge themselves in learning environments. Others say that they appreciate family yet don't work to build, maintain, or repair relationships. The more you consciously fill your days with people and experiences you value, the more you'll enjoy being yourself. Living meaningful days, over time, leads to living an inspired life.

You cannot operate on empty and live fully. People today are often more concerned about recharging their devices than themselves. For peak performance, it is essential that you cherish your body, mind, and spirit. *Make time for physical activity*—daily vigorous exercise will boost your energy, increase your focus, and have you feeling awesome (you'll never regret a workout that you complete). *Get proper sleep*—having the discipline to limit your distractions before bed and get a full night's rest will ensure that you are ready to produce at superstar levels. *Fuel your body with real food*—developing world-class qualities requires energy; eating a healthy, balanced diet will give you the fuel needed to go the extra mile. *Build downtime into your day*—personal time allows you to de-stress and relax. In a world full of distraction, carving out ten minutes of alone time for meditation, journal writing, or reflection will bring clarity to your actions, attitudes, and life's direction. Find a quiet, comfortable space to slow down your breathing, thinking, and being for a little while. To paraphrase a Zen proverb, the moment we slow down is the moment happiness catches up. *Practice positive self-talk and visualization*—filling your mind with positive affirmations will lift your spirit and instill within you the confidence to work relentlessly toward your desired results. Tell yourself that you are capable of your best effort, envision accomplishing your goals, and feel the emotions associated with triumph. Through the power of positive thinking, you can plant seeds of beneficial beliefs deep in your subconscious mind, which cultivates the majority of your thoughts. Self-talk and visualization can rewire your mindset in a way that focuses on positive growth. This whole book is about setting you up for success, so prepare your mind, body, and spirit for a healthy, happy life.

There will only ever be one of you, so give the world your best. Know that while you experience moments of development and achievement, other people will appear like weeds in an attempt to spoil your growth. They will doubt your actions in an attempt to break you down and shatter your confidence. Pay them no mind. These selfish tactics, often triggered by envy, likely mean that you're on the right track. Stay the course by continuing to lead your best life. The people who matter will love you, and more importantly, you'll love yourself. That's the truth.

Reflection and Self-Awareness Opportunity

1) Which statement best describes how authentic you are in your social groups?
    a) I always find it hard to be myself.
    b) I sometimes find it hard to be myself.
    c) I am usually comfortable being myself.
    d) I am always comfortable being myself.

If you answered A or B, what could you try doing to improve this situation?

2) Take a few minutes, distraction free, to think about your recent attitudes and actions. What do they reveal about your life and its current direction? Are they true to your values?

3) How prepared is your mind, body, and spirit for a life well lived? Circle the components of a healthy lifestyle that you could improve upon:
    a) Physical activity
    b) Sleep
    c) Healthy eating
    d) Downtime
    e) Positive self-talk and visualization

Try creating a SMART goal, along with actions, for any areas you identified. Refer to chapter 7 for help with this activity.

27

Be Inspirational

Each person must live their life as a model for others.

—Rosa Parks

An inspired life is a life with purpose. What inspires us can come from anywhere: nature, art, music, science, athletics, or anything else can motivate us to act in extraordinary ways and accomplish amazing feats. Observing other people is also a tremendous source of inspiration; the actions, attitudes, or attributes of particular individuals can lift our spirits. Whether it is a celebrity, friend, family member, or stranger, I'm sure somebody lives life in a way that inspires you. **Inspiration is a beautiful gift; it is great to receive, but giving the gift of inspiration to others is even more gratifying.**

A daily commitment to living your best life will make you an inspirational leader. You do not have to be famous or do something extravagant. One act of kindness, courage, or compassion can make others want to better themselves because of you. Your actions just might be the inspiration someone needs—you never know what struggles people are facing in their own lives. To quote civil rights activist Maya Angelou, "Try to be a rainbow in someone else's cloud," and let your actions bring light and beauty into someone's world.

School offers you a multitude of opportunities to inspire others every day. You can act as an inspiration by doing the following:

- Trying your best
- Stepping out of your comfort zone
- Standing up for a person or cause
- Staying true to yourself
- Overcoming adversity
- Living a healthy lifestyle
- Pursuing your passion
- Showing compassion
- Helping others

And the list goes on. Living as a model for others makes you a leader by example, which is necessary because your generation will one day lead the world. You heard that right: lead the world. Your decisions and actions will guide and shape your life and the lives of others. It's a big responsibility, but it shouldn't scare you. It should excite you. It's an inspirational opportunity. Giving your best effort in life will bring out the best in others, who will then go on to inspire even more people. Imagine what we would accomplish if the whole world lived as a model for others. Thinking about it gives me chills. The world cannot survive and thrive without inspirational people, for they ignite the passion and effort needed to positively change the world.

Every day, continue to find inspirational motivation from others, but show your gratitude by passing it on. Live in a way that elevates those around you. Find a mentor, and adopt the qualities of those you admire. The world needs inspiration, and the best way to create it is to model it. The great teacher Confucius said, "When you see a good person, become like her or him. When you see a bad person, reflect upon yourself." By remaining mindful of your own behavior, you will encourage others through your actions. Not only will you raise your performance, but you will also live a fulfilled life knowing that you made a difference in the lives of others. You will give the gift of inspiration. That is a superstar quality if there ever was one.

Reflection and Self-Awareness Opportunity

1) Think of someone who has been inspirational in your life. What qualities or actions do you admire about that person? Try to adopt those qualities into your own life.

2) When you think of your life now, could any of your daily actions inspire others?
   Yes   No   Sometimes

If yes, keep it up! Write down your best actions so you continue to lead by example and inspire others.

If you answered no or sometimes, write down a change you could make in your life that could also inspire others to improve. Refer to the list in the chapter for ideas.

3) Tell those who inspire you just how much you appreciate what they do. By doing so, you will inspire them!

28

Create Positive Change

The secret of change is to focus all of your energy, not on fighting the old, but on building the new.

—Socrates

WHEN YOU BECOME excited about the changes you can make, your greatest moments await you. Living a purposeful life is a commitment to personal development, positive change, and meaningful contribution. The world-class traits discussed in this book, once developed, put your future in your hands.

I hope this book helped your mind wander because your reflections, along with your desire to improve, will jump-start your positive transformation. If even one chapter resonated strongly enough with you to provoke change, then this book has served its purpose. But know that consciously choosing to improve your life will be because of you, not me. You could read a million pages in a million books, and the content won't matter unless you decide it matters. Positive change begins from within. While some words may be worth living by, authentic actions ignite change and growth. Let your actions do the talking. What you do matters. You matter. Never forget that.

Personal development is a bumpy ride, so be ready for the ups and downs. Changing your existing habits will not always seem positive at a given moment, but the future rewards will be indisputable. Remember to start small. Focus on one or two modifications you can make and then build upon them. If you continue this process over time, you will wow yourself and others.

As you continue to develop, always focus on progress over perfection. Try to be your best self every day, but remember that life will happen and life is not perfect (although I try to live by the advice in this book each day, I don't always succeed—and I wrote the book!). Embrace the moments that make you human. There will be days when you don't bring your A game, when you put forth minimal effort, make bad decisions, suffer from setbacks, or feel like giving up. These experiences, once acknowledged, provide you with the chance to reflect, regroup, and rebuild your strength. Serena Williams, tennis champion and one of the world's greatest competitors, believed that "a champion is defined not by their wins, but by how they can recover when they fall." With a superstar mindset, the moments of struggle you endure will make your moments of success more rewarding.

You are the leader of your life—the fact that you made it to this page tells me that. You are going to succeed, and the world is going to benefit from your presence. In the words of human rights activist and Nobel Prize winner Malala Yousafzai, "Let us make our future now. And let us make our dreams tomorrow's reality." I thank you for caring about yourself, caring about others, and caring about your future. It should put a smile on your face. It puts a smile on my face because I know the future is bright.

You know what you need to do. The rest, my friend, is up to you. Make every day count. **Live kindly, learn continuously, and contribute meaningfully.** Be the superstar that exists within you.

Respect others. Enjoy life.

—Ryan

Reflection and Self-Awareness Opportunity

1) Look back through the chapter titles. What two chapters stand out as areas where you would most like to improve your superstar mindset?

   1.

   2.

Once you have incorporated these changes into your life, repeat this exercise until you develop the total package.

2) Final question: Which statement best describes you?
   a) Totally awesome
   b) Capable of anything you put your mind to
   c) In charge of your life's direction
   d) All of the above

Answer: D

If you enjoyed this book, please share it. The more we show others that we believe in them, the more they will believe in themselves. Together, we can create a culture where all teenagers learn the upside of valuing themselves, their time, their relationships, and their opportunities in school and beyond. Education is freedom. And with freedom, everything is possible.

For more information about Ryan Keliher and *The Superstar Curriculum*, visit ryankeliher.com

Made in the USA
Monee, IL
21 June 2021